RISE

RISE

How to Overcome Challenges
in Order to Live the Life You Want

NIA RAINER

NEW DEGREE PRESS

RISE

How to Overcome Challenges in Order to Live the Life You Want

ISBN

978-1-63730-359-7   *Paperback*

978-1-63730-360-3   *Kindle Ebook*

978-1-63730-361-0   *Digital Ebook*

To My Jewel...

Mom,
Who allowed me to stay energized with
Café Bustelo during my all-nighters,
this book is for you.

To my little buddy Boots,
rise and rest easy.

Vela,
Por ser mi inspiración en todo lo que haces,
Este libro es para ti.

CONTENTS

———

"The mind says dream. The heart says strive. The soul says conquer. The spirit says rise."

—MATSHONA DHLIWAYO

INTRODUCTION

———

You were born with it, and you will die with it. It has been with you for your first paycheck, your first kiss, and all of the best and worst moments of your life. Yet, it's the reason why some people are satisfied with their lives while others are not happy with theirs. It's the reason why we have amazing people who have invented computers, created unique art, started their businesses, and become the best person they wanted to be.

It is your mind.

Your mind contributes to the emotions of all of your wins. It also contributes to your feelings when you're uncomfortable, afraid, and alone. Whether it be your first day of class, being scared shitless during a presentation, or feeling anxious because you think you're not good enough for whatever reason, your mind is the most powerful and worst thing that can get in the way of your success. Your mind influences you to make some excellent choices or poor decisions that will affect your overall quality of life. Our minds are impacted by so many things that compel our actions. However, it's the little choices we make each day that collectively contribute to the people we are and the people we wish to be.

Our minds are influenced by the people we're around. Our family, friends, and those in our communities impact how we're going to live in this world. So when the world teaches us to question our differences and dive into our identities to explore them, sometimes it can be extremely overwhelming.

You can meet people at school and work and see people on television, but your mind is with you twenty-four hours a day, seven days a week. It picks up on those around you, which is a blessing and a curse.

Our minds teach us to constantly compare ourselves to others. Our minds teach us to limit ourselves to ideas of what we can be. Especially if you come from a place where you identify with multiple cultures, your mind is constantly battling different norms each day, which can mess with your confidence and ability to succeed. I say all this because our society teaches us to compete against others. Even though in reality, focusing on our own goals and paying attention to our wants and needs is essential for achieving meaningful goals and living the best lives we truly can.

We live in a time of instant gratification. If you're hungry, you can order Uber Eats or DoorDash. If you need a new outfit, you can order from your favorite store online. If you need to do some research for a project, it doesn't take long to do a Google search to answer some questions you need to know. What is not instant, however, is how we grow and develop ourselves as people.

It's the reason why only 8 percent of people in the United States actually follow through with their New Year's resolutions. It's the reason why when people want to lose weight, only so few people will continue to exercise into week two of their journey. The new age of instant gratification has impacted how we achieve our goals and aspirations. Although life can get in our way, the biggest reason why we miss some of our goals is because our minds prevent us from getting there.

Allow me to introduce myself. My name is Nia Rainer. My first name derives from Swahili, and it means "purpose." Throughout this book, you'll observe how being intentional with your purpose will guide your time and energy into the light. When you are intentional with how you wish to rise into the person you wish to be, you unlock new capabilities by unleashing confidence you never knew you had.

As we enter the 2020s, it's even more critical to be intentional with where you direct yourself. We live in a world where it can be very difficult to have aspirations and goals and actually follow through with them. Our surroundings can easily get in the way of our success. To survive the challenges of the big world, you must make space for yourself to thrive without asking for permission, make your voice be heard instead of just making noise, and solve the challenges that will impact those who come after you.

I'm thankful for the experiences that have allowed me to grow and succeed throughout my life; however, I've noticed these top three reasons occurred each time I couldn't achieve a goal.

1. I was in my own way.
2. I was not prepared.
3. I did not have proper guidance.

I want to emphasize the third one because this one explicitly causes the first and second factors. I was in my own way by letting myself think I couldn't do something because of what I didn't have. Things like: "Well, I don't have money," "I'm not that smart," "I'm black and racism holds me back," "I don't know where to start," "There's no one doing this who looks like me," and "I don't know where I can get access to information that will help me out."

I've said all of these things to myself, and they impacted how I went about trying something new. Sometimes this way of thinking prevented me from even trying at all. Sure, I may not always be qualified to do something, but every time I got better at something, it was definitely not because I sat on my ass and waited until I got "experience." I went into the challenge head-on and learned by doing.

It wasn't until I realized this one secret after studying successful people who made a difference in their quality of life that I began to change, and I want to share what I've learned with you. When you influence your mind to switch its perception of challenges, it's then you'll have the ability to rise to any occasion by unleashing your own magical concoction of confidence inside you.

Throughout your life, many things are going to be planned. Some things are already planned out for you. When you buy a cell phone, you enter into a plan to pay for monthly service.

It's the same concept when you subscribe to a subscription, rent an apartment, pay a mortgage for a house, or pay tuition every semester for your school. We should take control of things for ourselves though. When we create plans for our own lives, such as how we'll get a job we want or succeed at our next project, we plan for our successes. We also need to prepare for the roadblocks that get in the way.

But hold on, Nia—a.k.a., "Purpose,"—why is that?

Throughout my life, I thought my background, the environment I grew up in, and my experiences made me an unhappy person. But, in reality, the things that made me the happiest in my life were the life journeys that revolved around who I was. Some of my best memories come from being in college, even though I pulled some all-nighters to get some good grades and even some shitty ones I do not like talking about. For example, it was difficult for me to adapt to an environment where not many Black/Latina students like me—especially first-generation college students from New York City—were. Meeting some fantastic people, who looked nothing like me, on a Friday night in North Carolina to have a good time was one of the many perks of my decision to rise to adapt to a new environment, even if difficult challenges and conversations came my way.

Whether it be cofounding an awesome sorority chapter with remarkable women, starting my own business while in college, or being on an intense dance team in high school that caused me to shred pounds from sweat, pain, and tears, I have encountered challenges through every experience I've had in my life. The thing is, these moments are the reasons I've grown so much from being an antisocial asshole to learning to be a creative, sociable, and resilient person, as well as a person who appreciates the challenges and lessons learned along the way.

This book is written by me, but it's not about me. Sure, I may share some stories about me now and then so you can get to know me better. But again, this book is not about me. Instead, this book is about you and how to take your challenges head-on so you can become the best version of yourself. I've compiled some insightful research and spoken to bad asses in leadership, entrepreneurship, arts, and other unique fields to show you that the challenges in our lives are not going anywhere, but we can overcome them.

As you begin to read this book, be sure you have a pen and notebook by your side. Embracing the obstacles we have in our lives requires self-reflection and planning to get the steps necessary into action. There will be times when you may feel uncomfortable with some of the new ideas I bring forth, which will be normal. However, I ask that you read with an open mind. The way to overcome the obstacles that come your way begins when you use the best asset you have.

Your mind is your best asset.

Once we unravel what stops our minds from wanting to do the difficult, the challenging, and the ugly, there is only one thing left to do: rise to greater and better things.

PART I

UNDERSTAND WHO YOU ARE RIGHT NOW

1

LOVE YOURSELF AND YOUR STORY

———

"The most terrifying thing is to accept oneself completely."

—C.G. JUNG

SON HAN'S STORY

On the weekends, Son Han drives three hours from Houston, Texas, to the Gulf of Mexico. When he arrives, he puts on his wetsuit, grabs his surfboard, and heads to the beach. He swells with his board, spots his first wave, and rides toward the inside of the tube. All of his worries go away. After the weekend is over, he heads home more refreshed. As he heads to another one of these weekend beach excursions, he reflects on his life with me over the phone.

He shared with me that as a finance professional, one of his greatest blessings in life was growing up poor.

As the child of refugees, a first-generation college student, and a passionate surfer, he told his sister he's thankful for all of the obstacles they had growing up.

Growing up in Texas in a Vietnamese-American household allowed for a unique upbringing. He was in multiple ESL (English as Second Language) classes and did not have access to tutors or stellar extracurricular activities in his high school. What he did have were the strong bonds he created being surrounded by other kids in his ESL classes, the support of his family, and being able to believe in his vision.

He went on to graduate from the University of Texas at Austin with a bachelor's degree in business administration and completed his master's shortly after. He has had the opportunity to work at multiple companies such as Ernst and Young, Brainy Money, and KIPP Texas Public Schools. He's even had the chance to serve Alpha Kappa Psi as a partner producing personal finance courses for all its members.

But he said his time in the spotlight would have never happened without all the obstacles he'd been through.

During undergrad, he would often debate whether he should drop out of school to support his parents. Being one of the few first-generation college students at his university was frightening. "I had a lot of support from my friends and family. You don't have the time to go drink, to go party...I had to work nearly full time and study. It wasn't easy. I cried a lot. My mom passed away in January of 2020. Without her, I could not have done it." Being surrounded by people who did not share his experiences made him question his worth in the beginning of his college experience. But his humble beginnings and unique cultural experiences allowed him to understand the importance of appreciating who you are and the differences you have.

When Son reflects on his life, he realizes how much he values his difficult experiences despite the struggles they brought to him. After deep reflection and understanding that his differences were what made him Son Han, he learned to appreciate hard work and the value of humility. All of this allowed him to live a life of quality and fulfillment. These are the reasons why he can connect with so many people, be passionate about his work, and take the time to pursue his hobbies.

YOUR QUINTESSENTIAL FREAK

From the outside, it looks like everyone has their shit together. From seeing constant social media posts of everyone's highlight reels to wanting someone else's life, it's easy to think you're a quintessential freak, especially if you come from a household that models a different culture compared to everyone else around you. I grew up in a predominantly White area of New York City. While many people are familiar with NYC as being diverse, there was a lack of diversity within my area. Going to elementary school and being the only person of color there was terrifying for me. I would get made fun of by the White kids for bringing "weird" lunches to school. Even when I went to a more diverse high school, I still didn't escape the name-calling.

I would get called Oreo a lot for "looking Black but acting like I was White." On top of that, I lacked the confidence to bond with my family because I was one of the few Puerto Ricans in my family who didn't have a proficient understanding of Spanish. And because I only lived with one parent, I unintentionally built this terrible habit of being hyper independent, even though my mother always told me that help is a good thing. I thought I was a quintessential freak because I knew little to nothing about my ethnicity. I never made time to get to know myself for who I really was. At the same time, I would look at my Instagram feed and constantly compare myself to other people. Because I got so used to seeing everyone show their best selves, I thought I was always failing miserably. I began to feel sorry for myself, hate meeting new people, and wonder why I should even exist when I was always fucking up. It wasn't until I grew up that I understood the importance of loving yourself and how it can really establish confidence within you.

Son and I have our own paths, but we share a common experience. Everyone has a journey of self-discovery. Regardless of how your story starts, no one can define you or represent you. Although we all have our highs and lows, the story of how you respond and show up for yourself makes you unique, and no one can take that away from you.

You see, we live in a world where people dream of being someone else. I've dreamt that dream many times, only to discover it is a nightmare. Wanting someone else's circumstances, such as wanting to be rich like x person, wanting to be a part of the majority culture just to fit in, or even wishing to love as others love, is hazardous because wanting to be like someone else and not be you is harmful to the relationship you have with yourself. When you focus on your story, how you got to where you are today, and reflect on everything you have been through, you will begin to enable the most incredible power you have, and that is self-love. When you decide to love yourself for who you are, you can rise to any change and challenge and accomplish anything you set your mind to. As a result of loving yourself, you can enable changes in your life, which creates room for you to not only change but also grow.

WHEN YOU LOVE YOURSELF, NOTHING ELSE MATTERS

Making the decision to love yourself requires you to rise higher. You need to not care about societal standards or the opinions others may have of you. The reason why it's so difficult to do this is because we are wired to be afraid to be different.

In 1979, social psychologists Henri Tajfel and John Turner conducted a study on how people sourced their pride and confidence. From their studies, they found that people's affiliation with groups, such as social class and country of origin, was a significant factor in this role. As a result, the social identity theory was founded: When you can fit in with a group, you get your sense of social identity. In the same study, he also proposed that our brains have a normal cognitive process that puts people into groups and categories. As a result, our brains exaggerate the differences between groups and the similarities of things within the same group.

In other words, our brains are uncomfortable with things that are different. That's why people will always have opinions about you that you won't like. That's why people feel threatened by others who have a different skin color. That's why when we don't have similar circumstances to those around us, we feel inferior. Yet, it's those differences that we all bring to the table that make us who we are. Just from your existence, you are gifted. You were placed here on Earth to share that gift with the world. That gift that you have is fueled by loving yourself. Therefore, you have to make a choice to love yourself, your life, and how you got to where you are today.

Simply put, loving yourself is hard because we are wired to the desire for group belonging; outward love is so comfortable to us. From words of affirmation to hugs to someone reflecting the best parts of ourselves, being loved by others is something we crave. While it's important to know there are people in this world who love and care about you, you can't receive outward love all the time. But you are always available for yourself.

Self-love is vital to rising above your challenges and accomplishing your goals because you are the most qualified individual to give yourself love. You know yourself the best. You understand your emotions more than anyone else, and you know your experiences. As a result, you need to be able to love yourself for the better by taking responsibility, denying others' approval, learning how to forgive, and appreciating your upbringing.

TAKE RESPONSIBILITY FOR YOURSELF

As you continue reading this chapter, and reading this book, say this to yourself aloud:

I am responsible for my life, my decisions, and myself.

To love yourself, you have to choose to take responsibility for your life. By taking responsibility, you give yourself the power to provide yourself with better direction. And most importantly, you give yourself the power to change your life for the better. This allows you to make real-time changes that give you the ability to make the best out of your situation.

American talk show host, television producer, actress, author, and philanthropist, Oprah Winfrey, shared the following in her Life Class on OWN after reflecting on her childhood and her time on *The Oprah Winfrey Show.*

> *Being moved to Milwaukee and suddenly in a foreign environment for myself, I remember walking into that new space and recognizing that in many ways, I was alone, which is a terrible feeling if you're six years old. But I have always had the deep understanding that if anything were going to move forward in my life, I would have to be responsible for making that happen. And I know that to be true now and can articulate it. You are responsible for your life. And if you're sitting around waiting on somebody to save you, to fix you, or even help you, you are wasting your time. Because only you have the power to take responsibility to move your life forward. The sooner you get that, the sooner your life gets into gear.*

This is what I know from doing twenty-five years and doing thousands and thousands of interviews on the Oprah show. It does not matter where you come from. I have seen people come out of the desert walk across the desert, being born in the direst of circumstances, doesn't matter what your mama did, whether she did, or had a PhD or no D. What matters is now, this moment, and your willingness to see this moment for what it is. Accept it. Forgive the past. Take responsibility. And move forward.

DO NOT SEEK APPROVAL FROM OTHERS

As mentioned before, we are all used to what others think because we enjoy receiving outward love. But because we always have access to ourselves and not to outward love, we need a big chunk of our value to come from within. When we sacrifice what makes us happy for the approval of others, it gets in the way of our inner peace. Self-love means accepting all parts of yourself. Even the factors that may not align with the standards of the groups we tend to affiliate with. As a result, your love for yourself is more important than someone's view of you.

FORGIVE

I used to think that forgiveness was a weakness. I didn't realize the power of forgiveness until I started to become angry with the world. My experiences of betrayal, such as being bullied at a young age, being cheated on in past relationships, and only having one parent in the household, led me to become angry with everyone and everything, even the people who cared about me.

The anger I had from what others did to me was put onto people who had nothing to do with it. As a result, I've unintentionally burnt bridges with people who only wanted the best for me. Yet at the end of the day, the people who have caused my anger can leave this world without ever having apologized. The real weakness I had in my life was not me believing I was tough. I tried so hard to be tough and closed minded. As a result, I became angry, held grudges, and had negative thoughts within my head. In the end, my negative perception of life allowed one thing for the people who had hurt me: it gave them power over me.

When I learned to forgive others who had hurt me, I made a choice to stop giving attention to heavy baggage. I began to think about grudges in my life and how I viewed my journey to self-love in the same way airplanes give you a limit to how much your luggage items can weigh for a flight. You cannot go far on your self-love journey if you have an excessive number of heavy bags.

Don't get me wrong. Learning to forgive took me years to do. It was not easy to let go without me wishing for apologies from the other side, as well as me secretly wanting revenge. But when you want to love yourself, you have to release all the things that bring you down, and forgiveness is one of the best ways to let go of the unwanted weight. Remember, forgiveness is for you, not for the other party.

APPRECIATE YOUR UPBRINGING

So many things make us different. The factor that I want to shine a light on right now is one's upbringing; the views of an individual are created by those who surround them the most. This is very difficult for people to talk about, and

I can understand why. Depending on how you grew up or whom you were surrounded by, talking about upbringing can be one of the best things to talk about or one of the worst things to talk about.

There may have been some difficult moments while you were growing up; however, you do not have to view yourself as a victim if you don't want to. I bring up the importance of reflecting on your upbringing and appreciating it because of the power it gives you to move forward when you decide to take the next step in your life.

Regardless of how many highs, lows, or in-betweens, your upbringing is a part of your success story.

For just a moment, I want you to imagine a very unrealistic version of the world where you don't have to go the extra mile to reach your dreams. This sounds amazing for a temporary amount of time. Afterward, it wouldn't seem very interesting. And if you ever got a challenge, you wouldn't know how to handle it, and you would eventually lose everything you have as a result.

Regardless of how we think of them, people in our lives, such as our parents, grandparents, and other people involved in our story, are major influences. It doesn't matter whether these experiences are positive or negative. You can't go in a time machine to change things just because you didn't like how you were treated. One, time machines do not exist. Two, even though we are a product of our environment, we can't just make up the excuse that we were brought up in a bad way all the time. We cannot say to ourselves, "That's just the way I am," or "Because of the factors I faced growing up, I'm going to stay this way." Yes, it is correct that our upbringing is one of the primary reasons we turn out the way we do as people. However, that does not mean we can't grow. The past is indeed the past and should not allow our environment to trap us into a mold. Regardless of all you've gone through, you do have control. Your ability to control how you respond is what will make an impact on your life. At this moment, the past is the past.

While your upbringing may be the reason why you are the way you are, your upbringing should never be the reason you stunt your growth. Even though we were brought up in a certain way, it doesn't allow us to not be held accountable for our behavior; whether you like it or not, you have a choice on how you want to continue your life from this very moment. When it comes to upbringing, some people have really good upbringings, while others have terrible ones. Throughout our upbringing, we learn essential things from either our own family elders or even people in our own communities who allow us to understand different values and ethics, and these teachings eventually become a guide for us. This allows you to get support in times of struggle throughout your upbringing. You experience so much just from learning by doing, which is why it is essential for us to deliberate what influences are beneficial to our lives, and it allows us to see who we are as an individual.

THE POWER OF YOUR UPBRINGING

Robert J. Brown, author of *You Can't Go Wrong Doing Right: How a Child of Poverty Rose to the White House and Helped*

Change the World, said, "One of my greatest assets, was that I learned to love everyone, even those who did me wrong". Brown was born into poverty during the 1930s, only a few generations removed from slavery.

Despite growing up in a small town in North Carolina where he faced segregation, discrimination among Black people, and racism from other sources throughout his life, his upbringing had him surrounded by good role models such as his grandmother and his church community. The lessons he learned allowed him to take on great things later in life. He assisted in fundraising money from United States' businesses and humanitarians to support the American Civil Rights Movement. Brown has made moves within history. He consulted with President Richard Nixon on supporting Black-owned businesses to support the imprisoned Nelson Mandela, and he accompanied Coretta Scott King to Memphis the day after her husband, Martin Luther King Jr., had been shot. What kept him going through these tough times was that his upbringing was based on community, faith, and hope for a better future. Despite the challenges he had with segregation, he envisioned a world that allowed for change.

Regardless of our successes or failures, a huge component of what allows us to move forward is gratitude. Courtney Ackerman, an author of four books and a recipient of a Master of Arts in Positive Organizational Psychology from Claremont Graduate University, says that various things can conjure your positive feelings of appreciation or gratitude. When you affirm you have a good life, you acknowledge that the things that give meaning to your presence have value, such as your friends and family. As a result, that may guide people toward meaning and overall better health. When you apply gratitude into your daily life, it enhances your well-being, creates more profound relationships with other people, and overall improves your optimism for everything that lies ahead of you. With this, you have the opportunity to increase your happiness, create a stronger sense of self-control, and overall, be physically and mentally healthier. This is very important to take into consideration with your upbringing. If you come from a background where your upbringing may have been more difficult, it is only going to be even more difficult to appreciate the upbringing you had. Nevertheless, it would help if you took the time to enjoy the lessons that came from your upbringing.

Lisa Thompson, CEO and founder of Self Love Beauty, said that from her experiences growing up, she appreciated everything about her upbringing, even the struggles. Growing up without the influence of a stable father figure in her life, she learned to never depend on a man for her happiness, to never settle for anything less than what she deserved when searching for a partner, and most importantly in her eyes, she learned the importance of forgiveness. It wasn't that she learned to forgive for her father's sake, but rather, she learned to forgive for herself so she could let go of the pain. Authors Peter Vandor and Nicholas Frank from the *Harvard Business Review* discuss how those who grow up in cross-cultural experiences may increase individual capabilities to identify promising business ideas, specifically those from immigrant households. The discrimination a child immigrant may face within labor markets may influence them to seek self-employment. But overall, the challenges they face bring in more opportunities for immigrants to be innovative and creative.

While some children grow up in a new country and dread the discrimination, bullying, and challenges their families face, they are far more likely to be successful than the natives who live within that country by appreciating their upbringing.

Once you realize your power as an individual from what you have faced from your upbringing, you will soon realize you can do anything you set your mind to. If you really take a deep reflection of how you came to be where you are today, you have the power to discover what capabilities you have for future journeys.

THE POWER OF SELF-AWARENESS

When you reflect on your upbringing, you begin one of the most important aspects of becoming self-aware. The ability to understand your own character begins with not only understanding your upbringing but appreciating your upbringing and everything that comes with it—the good, the bad, and yes, the ugly. Regardless of whether you were raised in an unstable environment, faced bullying, or even straight-up discriminated against from members in your community, self-awareness is important because it allows you to see who you really are. To become more self-aware, you must recognize your story and reflect on all that it teaches you.

REFLECT, REFLECT AGAIN, ACT

Your story does not define you. It is your main teacher. Take a trip down memory lane and think about the people and experiences that made you the person you are today. Take the time to grab a pen and pencil and think about how your experiences made a difference in the person you are today.

Was it how you were supported by those around you? Was it how you were surrounded by individuals who executed in the work they said they would do? Or was it the people who gave you the challenges in your life that you reflect on the most? Regardless, it is important to appreciate where you've been to appreciate where you'll be. Once you have the opportunity to recognize where you have been, it is time to discover where you would like to go next.

TO-DO LIST
- Get a journal and write a reflection of your life so far.
- Ask yourself where do you want to be?

2

RISE BY TAKING OFF

———

"If you risk nothing, then you risk everything."

—GEENA DAVIS

The hardest part of getting a rocket into space is not while it is soaring through the atmosphere. Instead, it is getting the rocket off the ground that requires the most amount of effort. If you watch rocket launches from NASA, you'll see that astronauts and engineers spend a lot more time on lift-off compared to anything else. Since Earth has a little thing called gravity, a strong gravitational force makes the rocket stay on the ground. But with just enough rocket propellant, rockets can successfully launch into space; the law of inertia is enacted, which states, "An object in motion stays in motion unless acted on by an outside force". This law can be applied to humans, of course, as people, too, don't change unless acted upon by an outside force.

Whatever you want to start with, momentum will get you there. Constant motion that continues, otherwise known as momentum, allows you to move forward. In life, what will tick you off about momentum is that it can quickly launch you in either the right or wrong direction. And within that process, what allows you to stay on the right path is the ability to combine momentum with directing yourself through your value. When you decide on the need to grow, your life will change for the better, and it is through the combination of wanting to be better and wanting to take action where wonders happen. To rise, you have to take off. But what gives you the ability to take off? To build the valuable momentum you so desire, you have to actually change. Igniting change requires learning how to take a risk and learning from the outcomes.

RISK TO RISE, AND TAKE THE FULL PRICE

During any launch of a rocket, risk is always involved. Risks are also associated with every aspect of our lives. Whether it be asking your crush to go on a date with you or preparing for a presentation with thousands of people in the audience, it's not the action we're afraid of. We're fearful of the results we don't want. We don't want rejection, and we don't want to be hit with tomatoes because our audience thinks we suck. But to take a risk that may give us great rewards, the key to ensuring our chances of getting our desired outcome is through training for them.

James Baker III, who has served as the tenth and sixteenth chief of staff in the White House, said, "Proper preparation prevents poor performance." Suppose we are prepared for the risks we want to take. If that's the case, all you have to do at this point is just take the risk. In addition to the desire to take that risk, pertinent information is necessary to keep you informed. When you have enough knowledge about topics, you can have more confidence in taking a risk because you can project better outcomes.

Having a strategy when taking risks is essential to boosting your chances of getting the outcome you want. For example, frequently, people who become basketball coaches are previously basketball players themselves. In the crowd, it's easy to assume players are simply dribbling their way to the hoop. But that is not the case at all. The coaches are on the sidelines observing the game to create strategic defenses for their players. Their expertise from their previous experience as a player makes them qualified to take informed risks that will have higher chances of working in their favor. In addition to making yourself knowledgeable about taking a risk, being able to mentally say "I own my decision" makes all the difference. No matter how big or small, every risk has a chance of causing outcomes you may not want, whether it be failing your first exam in college or not seeing sales on your first business venture.

It is essential to learn from your failures. Making mistakes, no matter how big or small, and keeping yourself in check allows you to build resilience to make you ever prepared to move on to the next endeavor. A failure is simply a sign of a "not yet." Carol S. Dweck, a leading researcher in the field of motivation, visited a high school in Chicago, where she learned of a school that had an unorthodox grading system. For every class a student did not pass, they received the grade of NY for "not yet." The students who received a grade of not yet were motivated to do better next semester. While a failure has a connotation of being able to do something only once, "not yet" implies you have the power to improve multiple times when you have failed. By changing the way you look at the situation and by changing your mindset on how you perceive your undesired outcomes, you will create more opportunities to pursue your desired outcomes.

A CRIMINAL LAWYER TURNED COMEDIAN

Before his rise to growth, Elizardi Castro worked as a prosecutor and ran his own law firm where he worked as a criminal defense attorney. Every day, Eli was proud to walk into work because he was helping people in the courtroom have better outcomes for their situations. Yet, even though he invested a lot of time and money into law school, Eli felt as if something was missing. He desired something more.

From being born in Puerto Rico to being raised in New York, his intercultural experiences allowed him to share stories in a unique way. And through this process, he has sparked laughter in people. Since then, Eli has delighted audiences of all ages across multiple stages, and it became clear that comedy was his passion. Since then, Eli decided to rise by taking the risk of becoming a full-time comedian. And while he is much happier now with what he does, the road there definitely was not easy. In order for Eli to successfully rise, he shared with me the importance of wanting to grow for your own benefit.

"There are two different types of growth. There's one type of growth that is more of a professional development, and then there's a personal development,

which ideally would happen before you take the jump. It's kind of like before I take this big jump, you need to check yourself first. It's just like if you go skydiving. You don't limit yourself after you jump right when you're free-falling. You don't go, 'Can you check the clip? Is everything okay and good?' Where's your parachute? Always make sure you're in a good place to jump. And then, when you jump, you jump confidently. A lot of people think that jumping is the solution.

"I could say to myself, 'Let me get up there and jump, and everything will work itself out magically.' It does not, because even if you survive that jump, you haven't learned anything. The only thing you learned is that you're an idiot. So, ultimately, personal growth comes first. But that's hard work. Investing into your hard work is challenging, and that's when people usually get lazy, and they go, 'I want to see it. I want to focus on growth that I can see me like jumping off an airplane, like getting up on stage. Those are changes that I get to see, and I get to feel good about it.' If you do that, you should have already done the more complex work to get yourself psychologically and emotionally ready for that next step. It's about being honest, brutally honest with yourself. It's about introspection. We all know our flaws, and we all choose whether to address them or ignore them. And nobody knows that better than yourself."

YOU WILL LEARN FROM SUCCESS

After countless hours of calculations and preparation, the rocket has finally made its ascendance into space. Yet, astronauts and scientists back on Earth still have work to do: multiple parts are required for a rocket's journey heading into space and back. The same concepts of departure must be applied after you begin your journey to desired results. That's because while the most challenging part of launching a rocket is getting the rocket off the ground, you must understand that success is a never-ending journey. Therefore, you must change your mindset on how you view your day each time you get closer and closer to your goals. Celebrate all of your wins, no matter how big or how small, and keep moving forward. Understand that you have decided to rise to something better. That is a giant leap in itself.

THE POWER OF SMALL CHANGES

While significant changes can quickly impact our daily lives, it is harder to notice a small change we make for ourselves because we don't see their impact right away. For example, if you are an active gym goer and then decide not to go to the gym one day, it may not be a big deal. That is, until skipping the gym more often becomes a habit. You don't want to let that happen. Be careful to monitor small changes because they can lead to undesired outcomes. On the other side of the coin, don't forget that the more we focus on the small positive changes within our lives, the more success will follow in the long-term.

KEY TAKEAWAY

When you decide to choose the things that allow you to grow, the quality of your life improves because you choose to solve your challenges rather than turn away from them. To do this, you have to understand how to take a risk. When you can learn from your desired outcomes and learn from your unwanted results, your journey will rise to the next stage. Once you decide to grow, it is time to align yourself by creating your desired reality.

Create a vision board and find pictures that represent the things you want to accomplish, such as booking an audition or purchasing a car. Next, put the vision board where you will often see it, such as a computer desktop or fridge. That way, you can be motivated to take action on the milestones to your journey.

TO-DO LIST

- Create your vision board.
- Put your vision board in a place where you will always see it.

PART II

HAVE A VISION

3

POSITIONING THROUGH VERSATILITY

"If you want to be a great person, you must walk hand in hand and side by side with great people."

—DR. NIDO QUBEIN

This was the type of language Dr. Qubein heard from his mother from a young age, despite the adversities and circumstances they faced as a family. He lost his dad at six years of age, and his mother had to work day and night to support her son. Despite the challenges, Dr. Qubein grew up understanding that despite your circumstances, you still have the ability to be the best person you can be. When he was seventeen, his mother influenced him to study in the United States. He was lucky enough to earn a scholarship to a small college in Mount Olive, North Carolina. With a novice grasp of the English language and fifty dollars in his pocket, the boy from Lebanon left everything behind to do one thing and one thing only: pursue his idea of the American dream.

In time, it became very clear that the American dream was going to be very lonely. With no family support and being discriminated against on a day-to-day basis, there were many times when he wanted to head back home. Being in a foreign land where many people didn't understand his culture took a toll on Dr. Qubein. After not seeing his mother for years, it was hard.

But, Dr. Qubein remembered his mother's positive attitude. He remembered the endless nights when she needed to work to provide for him. He knew he had to keep going. He knew he came to America for a reason. When he saw that all of the successful businessmen knew English very well, he knew he needed to master English too. Every day, he wrote new English vocabulary on five-by-five index cards based on what he heard in class and in conversations. When he saw that businessmen worked long hours and took risks, he invested $500 in his first business. Then, after finishing graduate school, he began selling leadership material to local community leaders and spent seventeen hours a day working on his products.

Within a short time, his clientele expanded from the North Carolina community to over sixty thousand people in thirty countries. His English now gives him the opportunity to speak to different companies, as well as take on different business ventures, such as being one of the chairmen of La-Z-Boy Furniture, BB&T, and Great Harvest Bread Company. Now, Dr. Nido R. Qubein is the president of High Point University in North Carolina, where he is fueled by his dreams to lead the University.

POSITION YOURSELF FOR YOUR DREAM

The way you position yourself for your dreams is the same way you would go about buying chocolate. If you were to buy chocolate right now just for your own personal enjoyment, you would probably get something simple from CVS like a Hershey bar or Hershey's Kisses. However, if you were buying chocolate for someone else, you would probably go the extra mile to make their day, especially if it was for a holiday like Valentine's Day. When I say the extra mile, it would be spending more money, like going to Godiva to get this gift for an important person in your life. Hershey is bought for your own individual enjoyment, while Godiva is positioned to be a gift. When you get a Godiva box as a gift, you know that you're cared for. Whereas when it comes to Hershey's Kisses, you are going to buy those for yourself because it's a matter of convenience.

In marketing, positioning consists of creating an idea about the brand in the consumer's head relative to its competitors. The Corporate Finance Institute explains that the objective of this is to "establish" the reputation of the brand so that consumers look at them in a certain way. Godiva has occupied the minds of customers as a luxurious chocolate company. They have Belgian chocolates wrapped by hand to give you the luxurious experience of candy sealed in a golden gift box wrapped with a soft, red ribbon. This attracts people to their brand because they made the ability to put in more work to stay presentable.

Godiva emphasizes the luxury experience to ingrain your brain that Godiva *is* luxury, an experience worth sharing with others. For this reason, you don't mind paying for an expensive box of it for a treasured someone rather than some Hershey's Kisses. Godiva is successful in marketing their brand because before they focus on what the image of their product will look like on a billboard, they focus on their image in the most powerful place yet, which is your mind. Even if you prefer Hershey's over Godiva, that's because Hershey's branding speaks to your tastes. The well-stocked nature and low price of Hershey's make it super accessible and convenient for consumers who buy chocolate on a regular basis. It's probably also true that you might still reach for Godiva when you want to make an impact on someone with a gift.

If the people behind these companies can position chocolates with almost the same ingredients to be completely different ideas in their consumers' heads, then you have the power to position yourself as a brand in people's minds. Whether that be possible job recruiters, venture capitalists, university admission counselors, or constituents, you have the power to position yourself to be the best version of yourself for the opportunities you want to attract.

I actually had the opportunity to speak with Dr. Nido Qubein on the art of positioning. When he came from the Middle East to the United States with only fifty dollars in his pocket, he knew he had a lot to do once he arrived. Dr. Qubein knew he had to position himself to be successful. During our conversation, he told me that when you attempt to position yourself for business, you must ask yourself these three questions:

1. Why should someone do business with you?
2. Can someone else imitate what you do?

3. If you were in the marketplace to buy your service or product, would your business be the first thing that comes to my mind?

Dr. Qubein began positioning himself by understanding the language well and building a good work ethic. That meant studying English and reading and writing each day with the use of his trusty flash cards. When he graduated from his alma mater, University of Mount Olive, he started a leadership business using his knowledge on leadership to sell content like motivational writing services.

He spent seventeen hours a day building his business, and even though he didn't know English well, he used his network in his college and the nearby community to find people who did, and these people sometimes helped him write the leadership materials he knew business owners wanted. Although he had to hire writers in the beginning because his writing was not yet developed, he was eventually asked to come to speak at events for companies when he improved in the language. Eventually, he became a business consultant for companies and used his leadership background to assist companies. He understood that his experiences and his connection with building relationships gave him the positioning to do what he wanted.

"I knew that to position myself for success to be a great businessman, I knew that I needed to speak English and speak it well. Early on, of course, I had a heavy accent, but I knew I had to speak it well, write well, and use it to not just speak and write, but communicate well..." said Dr. Qubein. This was just one of the things he did to position himself to start his business ventures in America. This journey will not be an easy one, but it'll be rewarding once you find yourself succeeding.

What is it you want to accomplish in life? How will you allow yourself to get there? To position yourself for success, you need to think about what your goals are and put yourself in a position that will allow you to get there. For example, if you want to lose weight or become healthier, you have to eat right and work out. But any person who is passionate about fitness will tell you that running on a treadmill and eating salads is not enough. You need to work out your entire body, and you need to explore your diet by adding foods that will help you live a more nutritious lifestyle.

The diet you create for yourself, whether you decide to be gluten-free or become a vegan, has to be versatile enough to help you easily reach your goal of becoming healthier because you have little to no restrictions. When you work out, you should reach for completing different types of exercises for your body. So just as you must be versatile to reach a fitness goal, when it comes to your goals and dreams, you need to position yourself to become versatile to reach those goals.

Versatility can be defined as "the state or quality of being useful for or easily adapted to various tasks, styles, fields of endeavor, etc." When you acquire different skill sets and capabilities, you become stronger in your approach to succeed. As you take on the challenges of life ahead of you, it is then that you will have a tool belt of things to use in the near future. When you have this tool belt, being versatile is what makes you different from anyone else in the room. Best-selling author, Lauren Maillian, writes in her book, *The Path Redefined: Getting to the Top on Your Own Terms,* versatility is doing "whatever is needed to maximize value creation." This can include discovering new passions and new capabilities. Our ability to take on new things and not only enjoy the process but appreciate our growth and allow ourselves to become better is the key to becoming more versatile.

The way you set yourself up for success is by positioning yourself through versatility. To do this, be willing to go the extra mile to become good at what you do. For example, if you want to become a baker, take an art class and understand how the principles of design can impact how someone can look at your red velvet cake. Anastasia Soare studied architecture and applied what she learned to her cosmetics company, Anastasia Beverly Hills, to make it the multibillion-dollar company it is today. What makes us stand out are the experiences that allow us to grow in unique ways. Opportunities where we get a chance to learn something new can fall right on our lap without us even knowing it.

In addition to growing versatility with your skills, you can become versatile through your experiences that made you who you are today. Your story, being where you grew up, the languages you spoke, the foods you ate, and the challenges you had to endure to get to where you are today are also a huge part of being versatile. Dr. Qubein, as a result of being forced to learn a new language, became bilingual in English and Arabic. He then won a communications award. Also, Dr. Qubein said that without experiencing Middle Eastern culture, he would not have had the mindset to work hard and become an entrepreneur because that was one of the core values he learned growing up.

What's great about positioning yourself through versatility is that it gives you the opportunity to explore and try new things. For instance, think about getting a bachelor's degree from college. Even though you have to take classes that are required for your specific program, you still have to take general education courses to graduate. You might think biology class has nothing to do with your major in communications, but you now have the ability to say, "I dissected a frog, and that shit was gross." But more importantly, the experience allowed you to learn something new, a little nugget of information that you can tuck away into your schema and pull out later if it becomes relevant. You may never have to dissect a frog again but maybe that better understanding of biology will help you pitch something more knowledgeably at work down the line. There's no telling what value new experience can add to your future. That experience allowed you to learn something new, and it required you to step outside of your comfort zone to make that happen.

CALL TO ACTION

By being open minded, having goals, and taking steps each day to expose yourself to new worlds, you can position yourself for success by becoming more versatile. Each day, do not be afraid to think outside the box. Be flexible in your approach to your journey to your success. Oftentimes, the ability to become more versatile brings you more fulfillment and more success. To have this success that people do not have, be willing to do things people may not be willing to do. Therefore, as you reflect on your experiences, do things that scare you, reflect on where you want to be in the future, and make it a habit to learn new things.

TO DO LIST

- Do things that scare you.
- Think about where you want to see yourself five years from now.
- Make a habit of reading one book a week.

4

LEARN TO LOVE YOUR STRUGGLES

———

Struggling is not the identity. You must learn to live while you struggle, such that anyone who sees you can separate the struggle from your life.

—JOSHUA HOOK

"I feel like a failure."

Growing up, I fervently thought I wanted to be a singer. I tried to sing a cover of every new song I heard. I would go to sleep at night dreaming I was performing at a concert on my world tour. I was fascinated with the thought of performing multiple nights a week, being on numerous talk shows, and making music to be a successful artist. Having strangers scream "Nia" in awe of what I do was a dream of mine. I wanted people pulling my music up on Spotify and having my songs on repeat like I had SZA. How I felt watching some of my favorite performers on stage inspired me. It was all I could think about from middle school to early high school.

These thoughts motivated me to work on my craft. I began practicing songs at home, working with a vocal coach, and even got accepted into a performing arts high school to study vocal music for five days a week. Throughout this time, I was very committed to working on becoming a better vocalist. However, these few years only consisted of me learning techniques and understanding what makes my voice unique. I learned how to control my breath, how my posture should be, having the correct pitch, vowels, tones, and so on. It wasn't until I began auditioning for gigs when things began to change.

After carefully studying for such a long time, I figured auditioning would be easy since I'd spent so much time training. I was wrong. I needed to make time to learn audition material. Depending on what some auditions required, I needed to work on an audition portfolio of songs to pull up and make time to learn songs at the last minute. On top of that, I still needed to work on my technique as I'd been doing before I began auditioning for roles. Then, I needed to get to know people in the artist community, which was when everything stopped.

I stopped auditioning. It was so frustrating to me how the opportunities I would perform in would be based on what directors were "looking for." I couldn't imagine what it would be like for me to depend on getting gigs to pay my rent. Thankfully, I was still only a high school student at the time. I didn't have the thick skin to handle multiple rejections at once. Moreover, having to wait around to hear that rare "yes" come from another person didn't sit right with me. I began not caring about my vocal classes. During my senior year, I even tried to get excused from my vocal classes completely. I hated myself for a while because I felt I had wasted years trying to become something I thought I wasn't good at. Because I was surrounded by students so passionate about music, I began to disconnect with those around me to the point where I was counting down the days to graduation. Sure, most high school seniors get excited thinking about college and what's next, and I thought about that. But what I was really counting down the days to was the day I wouldn't have to sing anymore.

I hated myself because I thought I was a quitter. I hated myself because I had people believing in me, and I felt I had let others down. After time had passed though, I sat down and realized one thing. I had never really wanted it.

I never wanted to become a singer. I had just wanted to have the attention that singers get. I was obsessed with the results of being known, having songs to call my own, and even having the media ask me questions about myself so I could be famous. I didn't want to be rehearsing all the time, learning new music, or even going to auditions for shows I most likely wouldn't perform in.

But then, I became free. I let myself go from the shackles of my brain, telling myself I was a fucking loser. The reality is that for whatever you want to do in this life, you have to be in love with not only the highs but the process and the struggles.

———————

To find what you love to do, you can't only be working on things when they are easy. If I were to ask you, "What do you want to do in life?" what would you say? Would you talk about how you want to make a lot of money, have a cool job, and have a great family? If that's the case, what are you willing to struggle through to make that happen?

Everyone wants to live a rewarding life. It is easy to want to live a life that gives you pleasure. You want to be pleased by your relationships, your job, and how you look. But, how do you respond to what's going on when things aren't going so great? Do you walk away when you know there's work to be done? Or, do you make the constant decision to put your best foot forward and fight?

For everything you want to do in life, whether it be the job you want, the people you want in your life, and the activities you do, they will all have factors that will cause you to have struggles. Regardless if you are happy for one moment, you need to figure out what struggles you are willing to have to live the life you want. Are you willing to have a sixty-hour workweek to make a lot of money? Are you willing to be in a romantic relationship if you suck at communication?

Everything you think is supposed to make you happy all the time, will not. Even some of your favorite things will make you angry and upset. What you need to find out is what you are willing to be angry and sad about and what you are willing to work with to eventually be satisfied at times. The reality is that we won't always be happy. Everything that comes across your path will give you negative experiences, and it is only your responsibility to find out what struggles you are willing to accept to live the life you want.

Think about the challenges you are willing to accept. Anything you want to do in this life comes with challenges, especially with becoming a musician. The constant rejection, always being asked to sing in unorthodox locations, and the constant need to rehearse and rehearse without always seeing the results that you want was not the path for me.

One of my favorite authors, Mark Manson, talks about this in his book, *The Subtle Art of Not Giving a Fuck*. To be happy in life, it requires growing from your problems. He says for any problem, "...the solution lies in the acceptance and active engagement of that negative experience—not the avoidance of it, not the salvation from it." The ability to have a pain-free life is impossible. But what is possible is having the opportunity to choose your pain.

HOW DO YOU KNOW IF IT'S WORTH IT?

The key to success is more than just hard work. Instead, it is the power of consistency that allows you to move forward. The challenge that comes from being involved in multiple projects is that people are very focused on the results at the end. While this may work for some people, it is important to recognize that we are going to face difficulties for a lot of projects we handle. The issue that lies along with our projects is that if you take on something you don't enjoy, you'll want to drop it, and then you're going to want to get into the spiral of regret. You're going to ask yourself, "Why didn't I continue? Why didn't I persist?" The solution is that instead of focusing on the end result, you must focus on the journey that lies ahead of you. By creating a new perspective on how you view struggles, you will be more likely to go after your goals after you face hardship. Yes, rewards are great. Imagining results are even better. But you won't always get results, and to become better, know that you won't be capable of being rewarded each day. When this happens, know whether you are capable of bringing results right away. If results do not come right away, does thinking about the final reward inspire you so much that you want to continue working? Do the challenges you face within your daily life allow you to keep on pushing forward the next day? If you can answer those questions, then you understand the power of appreciating your struggles.

People fail for a few reasons. One is because they lack passion. Another reason is they lack execution. Finally, they either lack the skill or the desire to learn the skills to make that happen. Depending on where you are with that journey, it is important to understand it's okay for you to lack knowledge, ability, or skill. If you really love what you do, you will go out of your way to get to the next level to succeed. So if you really love math, do not give up your math major just because you got an F on your last exam. If you really want to become a nurse, do not drop out of your nursing program just because your advisor said you would be better off doing something else.

When you sit down and reflect on what you really want and ask yourself if you want these struggles, that's when you can figure out how you can choose the best path for yourself. If you are so confused about whether what you are doing right now is right, consider these three things:

1. Are you willing to sacrifice to pursue what you love?
2. Are you able to give one or multiple things up to continue with what you're doing right now?
3. Do you believe that if you create sacrifices for this goal, you will have a great reward in the long run?

Now, there may be some confusion on that last one. Just because you may be talented at something does not mean you can't struggle with it. As Kevin Durant once said, "Hard work beats talent when talent fails to work hard." You could be very talented at a skill, but if you're not dedicated to improving on this skill daily, your talent doesn't mean anything. Therefore, you must ask yourself if you are willing to perfect your craft daily, regardless of the natural abilities you already have or lack thereof. Would you be able to make an impact on others with what you want to do? In our minds, we love to think our passions are really for ourselves. While passions allow for happiness, passions also contribute to the well-being of those around us. Being able to pour love into something you want to do makes a profound impact on people because it gets people excited.

Best-selling author Mark Manson said, "Happiness comes from solving problems." Meaning a person's life is more fulfilling when they are actively creating solutions. That is why you can't rely solely on your talents to get you far because relying solely on your talents will eventually make you stagnant. If you don't find a problem to solve, it can actually be pretty risky. Psychologist Constance L. Hammen argued that people with a lack of problem-solving abilities tend to act on impulse when experiencing a difficult situation, further adding to the problem and ultimately leading to depression and other mental health disorders.

This is not to be confused with "No pain, no gain," "Hustle, Hustle, Hustle," or "Positive vibes only" mindsets. I would be lying if I said choosing your pain would allow you to be happy all of the time because it doesn't. In addition to recognizing your struggles, you can make time to take breaks, rest, and learn to step away. Throughout the time you are learning yourself and what types of pain you want in your life, you must recognize that it's okay to be disappointed even with your struggles. It is okay if you are not okay and if you need to talk to someone about your pain. No matter how big or how small, all of your feelings are valid. What's important to remember is when you are finding the struggles you enjoy, remember everything has a solution. Therefore, complaining about your problems, whether it be to yourself or to others, does not do anything about your responsibility to find a solution to your problem. It is okay to complain every once in a while, but do not get so sucked into your complaints that you never solve the problems you have at hand.

Even with the struggles we do not ask for, whether it's being a member of a historically marginalized group, other people's poor decisions making an impact on our own lives, or the struggles we sometimes we create for ourselves without even realizing it, it's all a part of us recognizing these struggles lead to our happiness. These struggles allow us to appreciate ourselves for who we are as people as we overcome things and share ourselves with others.

THE HONEST TRUTH

You must know you are going to die. Although the average life span of a human being tends to increase as technology improves, neither technology nor human innovation will allow you to live forever. But your purpose will allow you to have a legacy that will last forever. Hence, your decisions to pursue your goals must fulfill your happiness in the long-term. It is simple to fall into the trap of wanting to do something just because someone else did it or because someone is telling you to do something. When you see a live performance of talented artists, you only see the results of their long hours of rehearsals. When you see someone graduate and earn their degree, you don't see the long hours of studying they put in at the library to do well in their classes. When you see someone get a new job or promotion, you don't see the hard work they've done in their previous role.

Imagine a tree in a forest if you were to look at its branches, leaves, trunk, and bark. You may say to yourself, "What a pretty tree!" However, what you don't see below the soil are the roots. They are scattered and clench tightly against each other below. These roots play a massive role in supporting the tree. Not only do they absorb the water and nutrients from the soil into the tree, but the roots also ensure that the tree stands erect. The roots overcome the challenges of supporting the tree, regardless of droughts, floods, earthquakes, or lack of sunshine. You may not see a tree's roots, but that tree will not stand without them even though they are not visible at all, especially when they have their challenges. Your roots, in this case, are the successes from challenges that arise. For every goal you have, understand that there are challenges to all of them. Yet without those challenges, there would not be a goal to reach. Therefore, while you don't have to love the challenges, you go through them every second of the day. It would help if you find goals that have challenges you will enjoy in the long-term.

It may take some time to understand what goals you may want to achieve when it comes to goal setting, and that's okay. Making enough time for creating your objectives is essential. As you become older, understand that your decisions are entirely yours. Simultaneously, it is the most amazing and scary experience. No one is telling you what to do, and it's all up to you to figure out what you want in your life. When this is discovered, the freedom is exhilarating. From being able to legally drive, drink, purchase any product or service, or going out whenever and wherever you want, any action you execute is your responsibility. With this freedom, it's easy to take it for granted. However, know that you must want better for yourself to take responsibility for your life. And this happens when you make goals that guide you in the right direction. Goals that are guided do three things. One, they put you first. Two, they impact your future. Three, they allow you to grow, even when you don't feel like growing.

When you have goals that do these three things, you will find passions more quickly because the process will allow you to be your most authentic self. When you are your most authentic self, you recognize your abilities and get excited about the life you have in front of you. Guided goals put you first. When you create plans that have your best interests first, you will attract others who value your worth. Making goals this way will allow you to see who is meant to be in your life versus those who aren't. For example, don't study to become a doctor just because your parents told you to. Or, let's say you are the heir of a family-owned business, and you are expected to be next in line to lead. If you feel you aren't passionate about running the family business, talk to your family about putting someone else in the family for that role.

Goals that are created to focus on yourself or others will definitely push you to be challenged. However, if you cannot enjoy the challenges or the rewards, then it doesn't matter how much money you'll make or the clout you're going to get. Happiness doesn't have its favorites, and that's why you can have just a penny to your name and be happy. In contrast, you can be the richest person in the world and be depressed. It's great to do things that will make others proud of you. However, when you put anyone's happiness before your own, you will never win.

When you make goals that allow you to put your happiness first, you are taking advantage of your free will, which is one of the greatest blessings you will ever have. Secondly, the goals you create for yourself allow you to set yourself up for future success. All of your goals need to allow you to work on something for a certain period to create the result you desire. In that process, you will face adversities that will challenge you. When that happens, keep going. You're doing the right thing because your goals are meant specifically for you. Lastly, goals that are meant for you push you to want to do better for yourself; they get you to leave your comfort zone by allowing you to experiment with new things. This is important because regardless of your goals, know that you will become better by doing the things that scare you. Unlike guided goals, misguided goals place more of an emphasis on pleasing those around you. Know that to ensure you are living your life to the fullest, make sure your goals are guided.

Not only will you become a people pleaser, but you'll also be on the chase to fit within someone's perception of you. That chase is dangerous; you lose yourself when you do things just to make others happy. In addition, misguided goals keep you stagnant. Something can always be learned in everything you do. Do not replay lessons you've already learned from your prior experiences. You must decide to have goals that allow you to become better. Otherwise, you will miss opportunities that will get you to a rewarding future.

TRY NEW THINGS, EVEN IF YOU SUCK AT THOSE THINGS IN THE BEGINNING

Have you always wanted to skydive, paint on a canvas, or learn how to code? Whatever it is you want to pursue, try it. What's nice about learning in the twenty-first century is that you have access to everything by virtue of the internet. You can watch YouTube tutorials and follow along with something you have always wanted to do. It will be very uncomfortable at the beginning because your brain is going to resist the change. Your job is to resist this urge.

However, after you get used to the newness of the unknown, pay attention to the overall themes of challenges you face after doing something for a while. Do you enjoy coming through those constant struggles? Can you take full responsibility for your actions?

Having the ability to appreciate your struggles allows you to appreciate your life. Regardless of what your struggles are, they allow you to get out of your comfort zone. The truth of the matter is that everyone is always going to have struggles, and the least you can do is choose some of them when you decide to commit to something you want to do in this life. While figuring out this process, you are probably going to be unsure about what you want, and that's okay. This process requires trial and error. Therefore, you want to make sure you try new things and venture out. In that process, understand that you will struggle. However, the most rewarding experiences are the struggles you are willing to accept and take on.

As you reflect on the challenges in your life, write down in your notebook different ways you can learn to love your struggles. With everything you wish to do, be sure you take into account the struggles you may face along the way.

TO-DO LIST

- Reflect on struggles you have faced in the past. What did you learn from them? What would you do differently if you had this struggle today?
- Find something to do that is challenging. When you see you are struggling, recognize the struggle, and keep going for as long as you can.

5

OVERCOMING YOU— HOW TO DEAL WITH THE IMPOSTER SYNDROME

———

*"Never, ever, ever, write off anything you've
achieved as merely being lucky. You are
not lucky: you are hard-working and
capable. Don't ever question it."*

—CHARLENE WALTERS

Growing up in Westchester County, New York in the 1980s, Denise Soler Cox was one of the few Latinos living in her school district. As a result, she was unable to grasp the two coexisting cultural identities of being a Latina and being American. When she graduated from Boston University, Denise decided to move to Miami, where the struggle to accept her identity was put on hold.

One night, Denise met new friends at a bar in North Miami Beach. They began sharing stories, laughing about their experiences, and connecting as Latinos. Their similarities in cultural experiences, from having at least one parent from a Spanish-speaking country to being born within the United States, made Denise think to herself:

"My story is their story, too."

At the bar, Denise began to write down ideas from the conversations she was having with the people that night. While people had lineages from different countries within Latin America, the stories shared that night were all the same. From the struggles of learning Spanish at home and speaking English at school to what it meant to be the person to carry on cultural experiences to the next generation. These experiences, while unique to each person around the table, also carried the overall themes of trying to discover one's identity. Westchester made Denise believe she was one of the only people with the pressure of "not being Latina enough" by her Latino family and "not being American enough" by her American neighbors. The night out in Miami allowed her to discover what she later called "Eñyes," people who were born in the United States who had at least one parent from a Spanish-speaking country.

It was then she began to realize she needed to share these stories. She had a vague idea of filming these stories to provide a shared experience and sense of belonging to others. However, after two hours, the excitement she felt at the Miami bar was gone, all because she didn't believe her dream was possible.

"I do not belong in the film industry. I never made a film before. And who is going to care about this subject? Who is going to want to listen to this story?" she asked herself.

Denise's friends were excited for her and wanted her to begin the project. But instead of making the film, the idea stayed in her head for years. The idea was trapped by thoughts that reminded Denise of what she thought she could not do. But one day, Denise finally had enough. She decided she would start creating the documentary and was not going to allow herself to abandon this dream. Denise and her husband sold their wedding rings to pay the rent, and they also had their Mercedes repossessed since they could no longer afford the payments. She knew this film needed to get done. While Denise was correct that she did not have any experience in film, she realized her story was enough to move her forward.

After years of having interviews with Eñyes, Denise finally released her film, *Being Eñye*, a documentary project featuring first-person narratives from first-generation American-born Latinos. With the help of a codirector, a coproducer, and having multiple stories to reference, her idea became a reality after she took action with the resources within her reach.

THE IMPOSTER SYNDROME

The story I shared is one of the few examples of how the imposter syndrome can impact the way we think.

We tend to doubt our talents and capabilities with thoughts such as:

"This was out of pure luck."

"I'm going to get called out eventually."

"I am a fraud."

"I do not belong here."

These doubts always occur at some point in your life. But if your achievements result from your knowledge, work, and preparation, and you still feel it's not enough, you may have imposter syndrome, which is when you question your ability despite having excellent qualifications for the work you are doing. People with imposter syndrome do not recognize their achievements and experience mental exhaustion, which eventually affects their work efficiency and highly increases their stress levels. People with this syndrome, whether intelligent or not, usually feel like liars. However, their qualifications allow them to be successful in their endeavors. Those with imposter syndrome don't appreciate their achievements, ideas, and all of the things that would make them great at what they do. They live in fear that someone will "expose" them.

Two psychologists, Pauline Rose Clance and Suzanne Imes from Georgia State University, were the first to introduce the imposter syndrome in the fall of 1978. They studied 150 women professionals in education, health, science, and law. Their observations discovered that the women needed an explanation for their own accomplishments, other than their own talent and abilities. In 2020, researchers from the Stanford University School of Medicine also studied the imposter syndrome focusing on people in professional careers and found that the imposter syndrome is common in both men and women, with an even higher commonality in those who identified with an ethnic minority group. As a result, several of the participants in the research study were more likely to develop anxiety and depression later on.

While imposter syndrome focuses on people not feeling good enough regarding their qualifications, it can hold people back when it comes to trying new things too. When people don't even feel good about the things they are good at, it's going to be even more difficult to try something they've never done before. Hence why Denise Soler Cox had challenges starting her film in the first place. If you allow imposter syndrome to take control of your daily life, you won't allow yourself the room to improve, start projects you have always wanted to pursue, and have the potential to grow on a personal level.

Even though the imposter syndrome has only been dis- covered less than half a century ago, it is more common than you think. The National Research Council of Thailand estimated that more than 70 percent of people have this syndrome at some stage in their lives. While not everyone may be negatively impacted by the imposter syndrome in the long-term, it is essential that you find out whether or not you have it. The imposter syndrome can not only impact your overall confidence but make you unable to overcome your challenges by keeping you in constant fear. In other words, if you think you're a fraud, you may think you're preventing yourself from being exposed. When in reality, you are running away from your true potential.

Here are some signs to look for to see if you have imposter syndrome:

1. When you work tirelessly for professional training, it is good to keep learning or updating yourself. However, it's not good if you do it because you think you're not an expert in your field and should be (and you never seem to think of yourself as an expert in your area).
2. Another sign of this syndrome is that you constantly do extra work. Since you think you are inefficient, you must catch up. If you are well prepared and work hard, you are also likely to feel "happy."
3. You find it difficult to accept compliments for your work.
4. Even when you do nothing wrong, you apologize.
5. You adhere to incredibly high standards.
6. The fear of making mistakes overwhelms and almost paralyzes you.
7. You avoid expressing trust because you think people will perceive it as an unpleasant vanity behavior or an exaggerated compensatory response, as you firmly believe your work is not enough.

If you agree with three or more of these statements, here are some suggestions to help you break out of these habits.

KNOW YOUR STORY

How does the imposter syndrome start? It starts with your imposter syndrome story. Think about all the times you were by yourself reflecting on experiences you didn't feel good about. Was it about times when you were with your family and you were compared to someone else? Do you think about times when you were at school, and you felt you were not good enough because the other people around you were doing better than you on a test or an evaluation? The reason why imposter syndrome develops is because of our tendency to compare ourselves to others. The story that we think of and makes us feel bad about ourselves is a result of triggers. When you overthink the past and beat yourself up for your mistakes, it can be one of the reasons why you feel you are not good enough. Oftentimes, external forces influence how we think. For example, if you are known as the one who always gets good grades, it's going to be a trigger for you when you fail. If you are known as the one who always works hard, you will feel like shit when you want to take a break. If one of your parents said, "Hey (Your Name), why can't you be more like your sibling?" you are always being compared to your family members.

These situations, even though they may have lasted only a few minutes, are often thought about throughout our lives. They take up hours and days and sometimes even years to get over. These people staying in their own lane, or you feeling like you are going to get called out, or people making you feel like you are not good enough, is the reason why you have the imposter syndrome, even if it's unintentional. An example of this is if you were a first-generation college student and your parents did not have access to go to college. Still, you had the scholarship to go to a really nice school. You were surrounded by students who have had access to exceptional education opportunities their entire lives, so you may question why you were accepted into this college in the first place. These experiences, no matter how big, no matter how small, contribute to the reason why you have your imposter syndrome triggers.

While they may seem harmless and it may be easy to say to yourself, "I'm just going to forget about it and move on." They directly have an impact on the opportunities you may come across in the future. This is why when people get promoted to a new position, whether it be a manager, associate, or even CEO, people will believe they are not capable of what they want to accomplish. Triggers from these imposter syndrome stories will encourage self-doubt.

This self-doubt in our minds will contribute to poor performance. You do not want your triggers to be the reason why you eventually perform poorly in your school, in your professional life, or in your social life. These triggers will impact your confidence level, and it is very important that you take a look at your triggers and not forget them but learn them. Your triggers and your imposter syndrome story are the most important factors to reflect on for you to grow from the imposter syndrome. Once you have understood your story and your triggers, you are able to create a new narrative for yourself.

CHOOSE AND REWRITE YOUR STORY

Remember when I said your story and your triggers are still going to be here? That is because we are not going to get rid of our stories or triggers to treat imposter syndrome. Rather, we are going to rewrite them.

When you think about your triggers and your story about how you have encountered imposter syndrome, it is simply a story that needs to be written and rewritten. When it comes to levels of the imposter syndrome, something is always missing. It is not a complete story, and that is the reason why you have triggers. Every writer knows there are multiple ways to write a story. The most meaningful stories in this world are the ones that allow you to be inspired and to take action.

You must do the same thing with your imposter syndrome. You will utilize your triggers and your story to recognize positive characteristics that support the idea that you are capable. You are enough. You deserve all the accomplishments you have accomplished, and you are intelligent and witty enough to be where you are today.

For example, during high school, I auditioned for a dance team. On average, many of the girls I auditioned with had over ten years of intensive dance experience, as well as having been to multiple auditions. I, however, only had three years of dance experience. From the moment I stepped into the audition room, I did not think I would make the team. Since many of the girls had more experience than me, I did not believe I had it in me to do well at this audition. However, I didn't walk out of the audition. I performed the choreography that was taught at the audition, and I said to myself, "Whatever happens, happens."

Two days later, I got the call that I made the team. While I was excited, I thought to myself, "Why me?" There were some girls who had more qualifications than me. I could not stop thinking about it, especially since I swore I messed up the choreography a few times that day. (My friend who auditioned with me said I didn't, but to this day I still don't believe her.) After the first day of practice, my choreographer (let's call him Dan) told me he liked what I brought to the team.

"Well, what do you mean by that?" I asked.

Dan mentioned many of the dancers had great technique, given their experience level at the time of the audition process. Still, out of all the people who had auditioned, I brought in performance.

"When you dance, you create movement. When this movement happens, you could care less if people are watching you or not. But, when you perform, you capture the attention of the audience. I can teach you movements, and with time, you will get better with practice. But when you perform, you bring out your best self. Being yourself onstage is something that I can't teach at rehearsal."

At that moment, I began to understand what Dan was referring to. From when I was a child up into my teenage years, I utilized what I had learned in theater, dance, fine arts, and from singing in multiple performances to perform well as a dancer. Given that I performed many times in the past, it made sense that he saw my ability to perform as a strength. To make sure I did not lack confidence when rehearsing with the more experienced dancers, I began to pour into my power as a well-rounded performer. Not only did I work well overall with the other dancers on the team, but I learned so much from Dan and the other dancers. As a result, I began to improve so much in my technique, which was what I felt would prevent me from being on the team in the first place. That same thing I worried about became my asset when I focused on the strengths I currently had. Also, the choreographer and the other dancers became a resource to me when I worked on my overall technique as a dancer.

When you think about creating a different perspective from your story, understand that it is okay to explore different perspectives and situations to clarify your imposter syndrome story. Once you think about your imposter syndrome story, you can identify a few things. You can identify your triggers, as well as how you can respond to them. When you recognize your imposter syndrome story and the triggers that come along with them, it is time for you to change your narrative into a more positive one.

Your triggers are what cause you to feel like an imposter. But, if you change your mindset on what your triggers are, you will feel less like an imposter and more like yourself. No one can ever call you out just because you do not know something. No one knows everything, and so people have to take the time to learn new things. This can't apply, however, if you are not honest about your capabilities. A real imposter convinces people they are someone they actually are not. In other words, if you tell someone you have more experience in something than you actually have, then people aren't going to trust you and will think you're a liar. For example, if you say you are fluent in a language when you just started learning it from Duolingo a few days ago, you are most likely overestimating yourself because you are still in the beginner lessons. Remember, you are capable of doing whatever you desire. However, it's important that you are honest with yourself, as well as the people around you, about all of your current capabilities and experiences.

Once this story is created, it is time for you to learn to speak your truth. When it comes to speaking your truth, it consists of thinking about your accomplishments and owning them—all of them. You don't have to think of them all in one night, but understand that all accomplishments should be celebrated. Do not downplay any of your achievements just because you don't think it's good enough. This may be a challenge to some because the usual response will typically be, "I don't want to feel entitled, and I don't deserve to have a trophy for everything," and you're right. You do not need a trophy for everything, and you certainly do not need to be even more entitled in a society that already makes you think instant gratification is normal.

There is a massive difference between celebrating yourself and rewarding yourself, as celebrating yourself can be an activity of awarding value to something when you've done nothing to deserve the praise. Whereas rewards indicate that you give yourself something as a result of the accomplishment. When you learn to value yourself, you will then begin to understand you are not meant to live on this Earth for the sole purpose of accomplishments.

Also, I'd like to mention that all accomplishments are accomplishments. Sure, some may be more exciting than others if you spent more time and work on them. But whatever you do, don't downplay your accomplishments just because a portion of success is still out of reach. For example, let's say you apply to a job that requires you to know how to use Microsoft Word, PowerPoint, and Excel. You know how to use Microsoft Word and PowerPoint, but not Excel. You apply with your resume anyway, and you get hired because they liked your interview and your willingness to learn. As a result, the company says they will help you learn Excel to do your job well. It doesn't make sense for you to beat yourself up after you got the job because you need to celebrate your work just for receiving the job offer. You also need to understand it is never too late to learn something new.

When you discover your truth, know that it is time for you to decide to get rid of the "imposter" within you. The imposter syndrome is like an infestation within your mind, and your truth leads to how you got infected. When you take the time to understand what accomplishments you have achieved in the past, you learn about your capabilities. Your capabilities allow you to identify why you feel like a fraud and that's when you have the power to discover how to get rid of it.

REWRITE YOUR STORY

Once you have learned about your story and your truth, you should now understand why you have imposter syndrome. The things that trigger your imposter syndrome, such as lack of knowledge or how people may have treated you in the past, are just a few examples. When you know what your triggers are, you can identify what causes you to doubt your abilities. Then, you are going to rewrite your story. From this point, you can choose and create a new narrative for yourself to follow. This narrative will allow you to become better at becoming confident, which will limit your self-doubt that stunts your potential in the first place. You want to make sure you take the time to reinvent your story.

First, rewriting your story consists of making the conscious choice to want to change. You have imposter syndrome because your mind plays tricks on you, making you think you aren't capable. The truth is that whatever you wish to accomplish, you are fully capable of doing so. Therefore, you have to make it known to yourself that you can do whatever you desire. To do this, you have to get out of your comfort zone and do things that scare you. Denise Soler Cox, who we met earlier in this chapter, set on creating her film, even though she questioned her ability to do so. While not having film experience was her trigger as to why she had imposter syndrome about creating a documentary, she went around this by bringing help to tell her story. In addition to getting primary interviews to utilize for the film, besides her own experiences as a Latin American, she got an experienced filmmaker to help as well.

When dealing with imposter syndrome, you need to know you can take the steps necessary to do what you are capable of and understand you are not alone. Talk to someone about how you feel, even if you do not have imposter syndrome from a project. Talk to a friend or family member, or go to a counselor to see how you can improve your situation. You will feel so much better just from hearing different perspectives on your situation. This can help you in the rewrite phrase because it can help you view your situation differently.

Next, know you can create your new story. Now that you know your old story and are committed to change it, it's now time to rewrite your story. Instead of thinking you are not good enough, rewrite your story and say to yourself, "I am capable, and I am authentic." Whatever caused your imposter syndrome in your old story, rewrite the situation by consistently making mental changes to prevent these feelings. For example, sometimes, my imposter syndrome kicks in when I am on my university's campus. I identify with being a first-generation college student and being Afro-Latina, some of the smallest groups on campus. As a result of the lack of representation within my campus, sometimes I feel like I am not worthy enough to be sitting in my classes. Even though being one of the few is not my fault, I must take control of my thoughts and feelings. Instead of saying to myself, "I am not good enough, and no one understands me," I remind myself, "I am unique, and I am writing my own unique story." This gives me the confidence to take advantage of what my university offers to me as a student, and I also learn to embrace my unique background.

CALL TO ACTION

Imposter syndrome can occur as a result of many things. But overall, the imposter syndrome occurs because your mind is afraid, always sending you signals to always be alert to getting called out. However, know that beating the imposter syndrome teaches us how important it is to love ourselves at all times. Regardless if we doubt our abilities, lack confidence in who we are, or even something else, it is possible for us to overcome our impostor syndrome. When you determine your current place, where you want to be, and plan for how you will get there, you will rise above the imposter syndrome and instill confidence in yourself.

In your notebook, think about what your imposter syndrome story is. Think about the first time you felt like you were a fraud. In addition to that first time, think about all the times afterward that you felt like a fraud. Ask yourself, "Why did I think this way?" If you were feeling this way because your mind was uncomfortable and not because you didn't have the talent to actually get you where you are, it is time for you to rewrite a new narrative for yourself. Being able to become more confident in your capabilities requires you to think differently. Therefore, in order to do this, begin writing your imposter syndrome story and rewrite it.

TO-DO LIST
- Write your imposter syndrome story.
- Identify your triggers, a.k.a., the causes of your impostor syndrome.
- Internalize that you need to get rid of the imposter syndrome so you do not stunt your growth.
- Make the commitment to utilize your strengths to weaken the "imposter" within your mind.

PART III

NO MIND
NO GRIND

6

ASK FOR HELP

———

*"You are never strong enough
that you don't need help."*

—CESAR CHAVEZ

Imagine you are in high school again, and you are applying for college. One school catches your eye for a variety of reasons. Maybe one of the reasons you want to be in this program is because it has leadership opportunities that you love to take advantage of. Maybe there's a specific task you'd love to do, or there may be certain classes at the university that interest and excite you. However, let's say you do not meet 100 percent of the application requirements, such as requiring a certain GPA, requiring a certain amount of educational experience, or even requiring a certain amount of work experience as a condition. There may be a voice inside your head telling you not to apply. There may be a voice inside your head telling you now is not the right time. There may be a voice inside your head telling you you're not good enough.

But there are some things that should be coming to your mind in situations like this. Have you talked to anyone at that organization? Have you done your research? Have you had the chance to go on LinkedIn and find people within that organization to talk to? Or are you afraid of looking or sounding like you are too weak to execute your goals? It requires stepping out of your comfort zone. And one of the most common ways to step outside of your comfort zone is to ask for help. Asking for help is not easy. When we ask for help, we may think we appear weak to others. However, it is the exact opposite. Something you're going to love about asking for help is that you can create higher quality results that will get you even further when executing your goals. By creating a habit of asking for help, you are taking advantage of your community and the resources it has to offer you, as well as lowering the chance of making mistakes that have already been made by those around you.

THE CONSEQUENCES OF NOT ASKING

While you are sleeping at 3 a.m., his alarm clock is ringing. He gets dressed, eats his breakfast and heads to New York City while it is still dark outside. He arrives at the Rockefeller Plaza and heads to the basement, where his spot in the control room waits for him. As he goes over what the show will be like, he knows that even with an agenda, there may be the unpredictable. Nevertheless, he's not worried. Joe Michaels, the former director of NBC's *Today*, has been working on the TV show for over forty years. Working on daytime TV, specifically morning show TV, is difficult because you never know what your morning looks like until you're live to millions of viewers. From directing cooking shows, shopping segments, and weather forecasts to having unpredictable moments during livestreams (think the Twin Towers terrorist attack or the Columbine high school shooting). Despite this, Joe Michaels has had many successes, running the most challenging show ever to be produced on nationwide television. I asked him how this was all possible, and he said it was because he allowed himself to receive help.

"You don't direct alone in TV or film. You have a crew," said Michaels. "The crew genuinely has to want to work with you, and you can't fake that. They're the ones that are going to help you save yourself and make things better. I can teach anybody how to direct. I can show people how to work the cameras because that's 20 percent of the job. The other 80 percent of the job is getting everyone to work with you and want to be there and do a really good job." So often, it's effortless to make people think managers, entrepreneurs, and people within the business are always at the top of their game. They make it seem like they have it all together, even though in reality, there is a gaggle of people backing them up. Being able to convey that they could do everything independently can mess with people. However, that is not the case.

Whether you are a seasoned professional or an intern, you will always set yourself up for failure by not asking for help. It is impossible to fully understand everything in this world, even if you specifically decide to focus on your specialty in a career such as Joe's. Joe had to work with other producers, the camera crew, and the anchors every day to create a good show. "There is no way you can run a multifaceted show like NBC *Today* all by yourself. You can switch the cameras around, and you can cue commercials. But you can't manage the chaos that goes on in the control room by yourself." He learned the importance of teamwork very quickly and understood the value of working, receiving help, and asking for help at the same time.

International marketing communications advisor Denise Fey conducted a one-month experiment, where she required herself to ask for help every day. Her results identified that people were genuinely willing to offer support. And if for whatever reason, they could not help her, they directed her to someone else who could. When she asked why people were so willing to help her, their response was they were happy to help. The ability to ask for help opens so many doors for you because asking for help genuinely makes people feel good. Helping people helps people. When you allow people to showcase their skills to you, you not only give them internal satisfaction but also build a new relationship.

Growing up as an only child, I was a timid kid, and I didn't talk much. My mother had to order my food at the restaurant because I was too shy to speak to the waiter. As I've gotten older, I've noticed that it has become tough for me to ask for help. As a first-generation college student, I had to work twice as hard to succeed. Besides the fact that I did not have the prior knowledge of college life like my peers did, I also did not dare to ask for help when I was struggling. Not asking for help, whether it be not going to a professor's office hours when I had a question because I thought it was a "stupid question to ask," to not seeing my advisor as often, set me back for a while.

If there's one thing I've learned throughout this journey, it's that asking for help is one of the most important things that you will discover within your life, as it can set you up for more opportunities later. When I began to ask for help as much as possible, I felt more at ease with myself, and I also got rewarded in the process. I earned Dean's List for the first time in my entire college career during the end of my sophomore year. I accepted an internship offer at a municipal bond insurer. This book you're reading right now got better and better after asking for help from my revisions team and my peers.

Have you ever had a person who took pride in knowing "everything"? They just wanted to tell the world about everything they knew. Yeah, nobody liked that kid, and there is a reason why. In addition, acting like you know everything makes you seem cocky, and acting like you know it all will cause failure because it limits your growth. There may be times when you feel like you are done learning, but that is never the case. As Robert Reffkin writes in his book, *No One Succeeds Alone*, "The real rules of the game are never written down." This is because it is the individual's responsibility to utilize help from others to learn new things. Being able to ask for help allows you to learn the real rules of the game. By giving yourself the chance to learn from your peers, educators, and others, you know the game's rules that you will not always find in a textbook.

HOW TO ASK FOR HELP

To ask for help more, reassess your ability to ask for help. Are you too shy to ask for help? Do you get angry, anxious, or nervous when asking for help? Or do you just generally not want to ask for help from people? Asking for help is not easy.

But with proper practice, you can train yourself to receive more guidance just by starting to do the following:

DIVE INTO YOUR RELATIONSHIPS AND FIND A MENTOR

Taking the leap is the most important way you can shrink your fear of asking for help. Whether that be practicing in the mirror a few times the night before or writing down your mantras of what you are seeking assistance for. Learning how to ask for help is essential for you to become successful in this world. Also, get to know the people you are asking for help. The more you know about a person, the easier it will be to ask for help because creating that relationship with them will not be as scary. Do you not have a sufficient relationship with someone to ask for help? Build that relationship through the power of mentorship.

One of the easiest ways to ask for help is through finding a mentor. Robert Reffkin, the author of *No One Succeeds Alone*, has greatly benefited from having a mentor in his life. Growing up with a single parent and in a lower-income community, Reffkin did not have many opportunities due to the lack of access his community provided. One of the biggest lessons he has learned was from his mentor. Reffkin's mentor shared that having multiple opinions and perspectives about your work allows you to open your eyes and see how others perceive you. From having the opportunity to learn from his mentor, Reffkin learned that honest feedback is a gift. Many people hate constructive criticism because it is very difficult to hear. But after taking his mentor's constructive criticism on a frequent basis, he began to stand out from others in his college and job interviews because he improved on himself and caught mistakes before he walked into the room.

Asking for help by having a mentor on your side is one of the best things you can do for yourself. Because in the long run, it is what sets you apart from other people. Recognizing in the beginning that you do not know everything allows you to soak up more from the people who genuinely want to help you. The power of people genuinely wanting to help you is another reason why you should be asking for help. Minda Zetlin from *Inc. Magazine* says, "Not asking for help means not being connected." In other words, if you are always doing things by yourself, you will miss opportunities to build relationships with others.

Every position you aspire for requires someone to help you along the way. If you cannot ask for help or don't know who to ask, that is a sign that you are not connected to a community, which means either one of two things. One, you need to look for a community you can count on. Or two, you need to create a sense of community. The best way to do this is by showing up at a location consistently. By being at a certain location on a consistent basis, people will grow familiar with your face, and therefore be more interested in building a relationship with you. This happens a lot at school, work, church, and community centers since this is where people spend a lot of time on a daily basis. However, if you're consistently showing up to locations similar to these and you think that you don't have the ability to build relationships with people at these locations, don't be afraid to dig deeper.

Take advantage of your hobbies to guide you to places you would have never thought of. For example, if you are interested in art, go to art galleries more often. If you are an animal lover and you have a pet dog, begin walking your dog at the dog park more often rather than just walking your dog around the block. You can create a sense of community with other dog owners just by consistently showing up.

Once you create some familiarity with your face, your face will become friendlier to others. In addition, when you attempt to build relationships with the familiar faces around you, there will always be someone within your reach who's willing to help you, and if they can't help you directly, they will guide you to someone who will.

BE INTENTIONAL

Let's be real, y'all. People are busy. Whether it's tackling life as a professional, student, parent, or something else, sometimes the people you desire help from are insanely busy and in-demand. Therefore, it is important that every time you ask for help, you make it clear to the person why you're asking them for help.

To do this, you must ask yourself what is it that you need assistance with. Is it that you are in need of assistance with a project? Do you need advice or mentorship? These are the kind of questions you need to think about when you begin asking people for help. When you do so, not only will the helper be able to identify whether or not they can actually fulfill your request, but you will also be prepared to pinpoint where exactly you lack confidence in a certain area. If you do this well, you will be able to walk out of the room confident enough to take on any challenge coming your way.

When you understand what you need assistance with, you can best figure out who would be the best fit to help you. It does not need to be someone with a big title such as boss or manager. Even your friends, family, and fellow peers can assist in your endeavors. If you have never met this person before, message them and ask if they have five to ten minutes to talk. Give them a heads up before and during the call about what they can expect from you when it comes to extra help. Otherwise, the person who you want to help you may come into the call blind and won't know what to do.

After you find someone who has the capabilities to help you, it is important that you make the ask. With the ask, you have to be specific and direct with the helper so they know what you expect from them. Make the ask for help, whether it be something small, such as asking for a hug, or having someone help you with a business decision. These are all forms of asking for help. Regardless of the price tag, know that as long as you are specific with your ask, you'll definitely get the results you are looking for.

AND GUESS WHAT?

You're going to hear the word "no" a lot. Sometimes it's not going to be a direct no. Sometimes it may sound like, "I'm sorry. I can't help you," or "This isn't a good time." Anytime you hear an answer not related to "yes" it is going to be disappointing. The truth is, not everyone can help you directly. Don't take it personally, though. While the person may say no to your request, remember they are not saying no to you. That person is saying no to the task you are requesting assistance for, and not everyone is equipped to assist you directly. Therefore, it's important that you do not take someone's "no" personally.

When you grasp the fact that not everyone can help you directly, understand that you still need to respond well to the situation. One of the most important things to know about asking for help is that asking for help builds character. Even when you do not get the help you need, you are still putting yourself out there and being vulnerable with another person. Therefore, be mindful that if you learn to respond to rejection well, it will pay off over time. This is because while you may get rejected when it comes to receiving help from them, the person you asked for help might be able to guide you to someone who can help. This alone, while it may not be the original plan you had in mind, can still put you on the route to getting the help you need.

SHOW GRATITUDE TO THOSE WHO DO HELP YOU

When you express gratitude, you are making an important statement to those around you. Gratitude is the fuel for receiving, especially when it comes to asking for help. Therefore, once you do ask for help and get the assistance you need, make sure you make it known to that person. People love to feel good, and so when you thank someone who has helped you, you remind them that their assistance was appreciated. This is especially important for you to consider because every time someone goes out of their own way to help you, remind yourself of two things. They didn't have to help you; they chose to help you. And the effort this person took to help you took time. Out of all currencies, time is something you will never get back.

Robert Emmons, the world's leading scientific expert on gratitude, said gratitude is a "social emotion." People who practice gratitude see how they have been positively impacted by other people, and people who receive gratitude often see the positive impacts as well. Therefore, every time someone does something for you after you have asked for help, remember to practice gratitude with that person. One of the best ways to do this is by making a habit of creating thank-you notes for people who have helped you.

To write a thank-you note, write a recollection of what this person did for you, and show your appreciation for it. Don't just say, "Thanks for your time." You'll want to be specific in your writing to make your note personalized. Whether it would be someone who gave you feedback on your college admissions essay, gave you advice, or even just allocated time on their schedule just for you to talk about what's going on, be detailed enough in the thank-you note to create authenticity. These thank-you notes show a higher level of gratitude that builds a deeper relationship with that person. So, if you write them well, you may be more fulfilled with your life as well as your relationships.

CALL TO ACTION

Asking for help is not a weakness. Rather, it is a sign of strength. When you admit you don't know everything, and when you display your vulnerability with others, you give others the opportunity to share their talents with you. As a result, you create the opportunity to invest more time in your relationships, as well as get guidance on how to succeed within different areas of your life. Be sure to get into the habit of asking for help by building your current or new relationships, be specific with your requests, and be grateful to those who help you. (Yes, even if they did not help you directly.)

TO-DO LIST
- Make a list of things you need help on.
- Show up to a place consistently and create connections.
- Build relationships with the people you meet.
- Ask for help with intent.
- When you do receive this help, make sure you express gratitude by writing a thank-you note.

7

DON'T LET YOURSELF BURN OUT

———

"Burnout is what happens when you try to avoid being human for too long."

—MICHAEL GUNGOR

Burnout left her lying in her home office in a pool of blood.

On April 6, 2007, Arianna Huffington collapsed in her home office due to exhaustion and poor sleeping habits. After hitting her head on her desk, cutting her eye, and breaking her cheekbone, she asked herself whether having a news company was worth having multiple sleepless nights. After numerous doctors' appointments and finding no underlying medical conditions, many doctors asked about her personal life. As the cofounder of the successful news aggregator, the *Huffington Post*, she worked eighteen hours a day with her husband with no breaks. She was making a lot of money, and the company was growing incredibly quickly. Yet, she failed to enjoy her success because she was too tired to see it all. On April 6, 2007, Huffington had a wake-up call. She quickly discovered that if she wanted to be successful, she needed to put herself in a position to enjoy it. Ever since then, she has been committed to ending burnout and focusing on having an existence where she thrives instead of just survives.

THE BEGINNING OF THE BURN

It's so easy to forget we are human. We've all had our moments when we stayed up late to work on something, or even worse, when we've had to pull an all-nighter just to get that essay or project done for the next day. If you have ever avoided sleep to work on something and gotten stressed out as a result, you are not alone. What you are experiencing is one of the ways people can experience burnout, which can be an actual diagnosis.

What is burnout, you might ask? *Psychology Today* defines burnout as "a state of emotional, mental and often physical exhaustion brought on by prolonged or repeated stress." It is the result of working long hours, multitasking, or overall losing control of how your responsibilities are carried out, whether at home or at your job.

During the 1970s, American psychologist Herbert Freudenberger established the term "burnout" from observing exploited workers at a health facility in New York. He described burnout as excessive fatigue from highly stressful situations. Over time, burnout became utilized to describe broader feelings of stress from low-stress levels to high ones. When you feel like you're inefficient and have a habit of becoming excessively tired, it is because your energy levels have decreased. As a result, there will be a decrease in productivity levels with the addition of significant changes in your mood.

While burnout is very difficult to deal with, you're definitely not alone if you have experienced it. In a recent survey completed by Gallup, they surveyed over 7,500 full-time employees about burnout. Based on their results, 23 percent of those workers said they were more burned out than usual, with an additional 44 percent reporting they are burned out on an occasional basis. Dr. Juli Fraga, a psychologist and writer from the University of California at Berkeley, said those who are frequently exposed to intense stress levels can get burnout. College students can be exposed to burnout due to the intense number of assignments given. If your career is very intense, such as being a doctor or nurse, or you're a high-level business executive, you're very vulnerable to experiencing burnout as well due to pressure. Lastly, if you know you are one of those people who identifies as a "perfectionist" and always needs to be in control, then you can experience burnout too!

LET OUT THE BURN

It's one thing to have occasional stress and tiredness. However, when you are experiencing high levels of stress causing burnout, your physical and psychological health decreases. Researchers from Gallup also say those who burn out are 63 percent more likely to take a sick day, as well as 23 percent more likely to visit the emergency room. This decreases your quality of life as it does not allow you to be well-maintained. The feeling of constantly being on the edge isn't reasonable as it literally does not allow you to feel good within your own body.

However, burnout does not only affect your mental and physical well-being. It also impacts the well-being of others. If you do not have the mental capacity to be in a good mood to talk to somebody or remember all the things you need to for a meeting, you won't be the only one affected by the burnout you are facing. Those who are burned out sometimes take their stress out on people who don't even deserve it. As a result of neglecting your well-being, burnout can really change the person you are into someone you do not want to be. Yes, you may aspire to be multiple things in life, such as an entrepreneur and student. However, keep in mind that you want to see the results and the rewards of your hard work. You cannot enjoy the rewards if you are too busy working on your goals all the time. It's not a surprise if you've been burnt out because of the culture that engraves hustle culture into our experiences.

Some people may believe that overworking is a sign they are dedicated to their role. Hashtags such as #sleepisforlosers, #riseandgrind, and #grindneverstops undermine the fact that, as humans, we have limits. Thinking it's okay to hustle all the time will eventually burn people out. And this destroys their mental health in the long run. It's easy to think the more hours you put in, the better. But as humans, there have to be limits so we can rejuvenate. Forcing yourself to wake up at the crack of dawn (with little to no sleep) to hustle and not allowing yourself to rest will cause suffering, not productivity. According to a study published in 2015 by John Pencavel of Stanford University, those with workweeks over fifty hours have a lower productivity level. Ridiculous work hours create employees who get less stuff done when compared to people who have forty-hour workweeks; these employees are significantly less productive.

In addition to this, if you are constantly busy with work, you are going to lose yourself in the process because you won't have the opportunities to hang out with people outside of work. If you allow yourself not to see your friends or family anymore just because you got a new job at a new company, please reevaluate your decision. No matter how much you make, nothing can replace family and friendships. Be sure to maintain your relationship with your friends and family. Because while a job may fire you, or a place of work may go out of business, your friends and family will be there for you after those things pass.

Gary Vaynerchuk, the founder of VaynerMedia, said, "If I'm feeling burnt out or stressed by work, it means I'm focusing too much on business instead of the big picture." In other words, hustle culture is bullshit. Social media may make it seem like it is fantastic to hustle. But if you are not genuinely taking care of yourself, you cannot enjoy the fruits of your labor. Although I am a writer, I have experienced burnout myself for many essays I've had to submit to teachers and professors. I've realized that the papers I did all-nighters for have caused me to get lower grades. When I would plan how to write my essays (whether that be once a day or a few times a week) and got them done before the big deadline, the results were more likely to be in my favor. It was vital for me that I utilized my resources to avoid burnout in the first place. Although it's not uncommon to be diagnosed with burnout, the nice thing about burnout is that it's avoidable.

SCHEDULE YOUR TIME ACCORDINGLY

Imagine there is a bank account that credits your account each morning with $86,400. It carries over no balance from day to day. Every evening the bank deletes whatever part of the balance you failed to use during the day. What would you do? Draw out every cent, of course? Each of us has such a bank, its name is time. Every morning, it credits you 86,400 seconds. Every night it writes off at a loss whatever of this you failed to invest to a good purpose. It carries over no balance. It allows no overdraft. Each day it opens a new account for you. Each night it burns the remains of the day. If you fail to use the day's deposits, the loss is yours. There is no drawing against "tomorrow." You must live in the present on today's deposits. Invest it so as to get from it the utmost in health, happiness, and health. The clock is running. Make the most of today.

—Marc Levy

Marc Levy, author of, *If Only It Were True*, writes this in his novel to emphasize the importance of time and the human soul. This quote is something you should write down and keep somewhere because like a bank account, we have the freedom to spend our money however we wish, and the same goes with time. When we make poor spending habits, we see the negative results of poor spending. The same thing happens when you spend less time on important things and more time on less important things. Therefore, to prevent burnout, you must be strategic about how you spend your time and when you use your time on certain things. The biggest things that impact our time are how we energize, how we fulfill our responsibilities, and how we grant our desires. It's important how you make time for all three of these things to be satisfied with your quality of life and prevent burnout.

The first thing you must strategize with your time is how you energize, as it impacts the other two things worth your time. If you do not have energy, you won't be able to fulfill your responsibilities and grant your desires. Arianna Huffington, author of *The Sleep Revolution,* said, "Getting the right amount of sleep enhances the quality of every minute we spend with our eyes open." In addition to making sure you sleep enough, you must fuel yourself with the right foods. I'm not going to tell you to create a dramatic change in your diet in one day, but adding fruits and veggies into your daily caloric intake can make all of the difference. If you are consistent in doing this, a healthy diet will follow in the long run. In addition, water is free, so drink a lot of that. If you want to get even fancier, put lemon in your water.

The second thing you must strategize with your time is your responsibilities. We all have responsibilities we like, as well as the responsibilities we hate. Regardless of whether or not you like your responsibilities, they all need to get done. Otherwise, they'll pile up and you're just going to be on your way to burnout. Therefore, be sure to schedule your time to fulfill your responsibilities, whether it'd be working on homework each night for one hour, cleaning your room for a few minutes each day, or walking your dog. Some tasks may be more enjoyable than others, so if you find yourself dreading a task, set a timer and work on that task for a few minutes. Then, when the timer is up, you can stop and return to it later or continue since you'll have more motivation to finish.

Lastly, understand that you are not a robot. You don't live just to eat, sleep, and work. While those things are important, how you grant your desires is the most rewarding part. Therefore, when you take advantage of using how you energize and fulfill your responsibilities, you have the opportunity to make time to do things you want to do. Make sure you spend time with friends and family, and if you have a job, save money on the side each week so you can spend it on something you really like. Whether that be something like a Telfar bag, traveling, or going out to a restaurant you enjoy, these moments impact your overall happiness. When you take care of your responsibilities and energize accordingly, you can maximize your desires in the best way possible.

HAVE A CREATIVE OUTLET

When your mind only focuses on responsibilities and rejuvenation, sometimes there is little to no room for your mind to wander. Your mind is curious and needs an outlet to explore. Therefore, having a creative outlet is the best way to do this. According to a study in the *American Journal of Public Health*, creative activities have "the potential to contribute toward reducing stress and depression and can serve as a vehicle for alleviating the burden of chronic disease." In addition, when you give yourself a creative outlet, you boost your confidence because you allow yourself to affirm you can do anything you set your mind to. As a result, you'll be less likely to delay your responsibilities because you'll have the willpower to get shit done. Also, having a creative outlet is just fun.

Below is a famous quote from acclaimed poet, Maya Angelou.

"You can't use up creativity. The more you use, the more you have."

—MAYA ANGELOU.

Making time for a creative outlet such as music, dancing, writing, or painting allows you to explore yourself in new ways. It excites you, and it enables you to invest in yourself. Although you will always have responsibilities you may not want to do, having a creative outlet gives you the ability to escape the world for a bit. As the world gets more stressful, having a place to create can lower that stress the world may put on you. The best thing about a creative outlet is there are so many ways you can be creative. Whether you take a dance class with your friends or practice an instrument during your own time, being creative can enhance your relationship with yourself and your relationship with others.

LEARN TO SAY NO

This two-letter word can make your life so much easier as you get busier and busier daily. We may not realize the importance of understanding our limits until it is too late. When you learn to say no, you not only become less likely to be burnt out, but you will be closer to becoming free. Saying no allows you to be in the driver's seat of your life. As a driver, you are expected to be confident enough to control your vehicle. When you say yes to everything, you are no longer in control of your own vehicle. This is due to the prolonged amounts of stress your body can experience from not having a chance to overcome burnout. As a result, people who have spent too much time saying yes often have higher chances of being depressed in years to come. Therefore, be sure to understand what your limits are as a person. While you can put your mind to anything you wish, understanding that you can't do it all makes a difference in becoming better at saying no, recognize that you are capable of putting yourself first. Even with a full glass of water, you can't keep pouring forever. The truth is, you cannot pour from an empty cup, and all cups need to be refilled.

CALL TO ACTION

While stress is inevitable, you don't have to be so stressed to the point where you are constantly burnt out. By making your well-being a priority over your job, school, or other people, you can perform well in all aspects of your life, giving yourself more opportunities to be confident. In the next chapter, we will talk about another way to put yourself first by practicing self-care.

TO-DO LIST

- Every day, make a schedule for your responsibilities and rejuvenation.
  - Incorporate eight hours of sleep
  - Incorporate times for breakfast, lunch, and dinner
  - Have snack times for fruits and veggies

- Delegate your tasks from high priority to low priority. Do high priority tasks first, and if you dread these tasks, put yourself on a timer.
- Plan a time to do something fun during your free time and keep it consistent.
- Find a creative outlet, such as going to a dance class, painting class, or music class. If you like it, keep going on a consistent basis.

8

PRACTICE SELF-CARE

"Caring for myself is not self-indulgence, it is self-preservation, and that is an act of political warfare."

—AUDRE LORDE

As a frequent traveler, you can find me at the airport several times per year. Whether I'm coming home for Thanksgiving break, making plans for spring break, or heading home for the holidays, I've experienced everything in the book when it comes to airport staff. I've had to wait for hours on end in the airport lobby because my flight is delayed, and I had to sprint to the other side of the terminal with seconds to spare because of safety checkpoint delays. Most of my time trying to make it to my plane is unpredictable. What does stay the same, however, is the process that comes after making it to my plane. As soon as I put my carry-on bag in the overhead bin, I sit down, buckle up, and mouth the words of the flight attendants as they begin their mandatory speech on airplane safety.

Before the flight attendants deliver their spiel, they inform passengers about what airline they're on, as well as the duration of the flight. While it does depend on your destination, all flight attendants share a variation of the rule on oxygen masks below:

Should the cabin lose pressure, oxygen masks will drop from the overhead area. Please place the mask over your own mouth and nose before assisting others.

Just like you are supposed to prioritize yourself to prevent health complications in these situations, the same concept applies to the topic of self-care.

Self-care is vital for anyone to thrive in this world. Matthew Glowiak, a Southern New Hampshire University professor, describes self-care as "caring for yourself" and "anything you do to keep yourself healthy in a physical, mental, and spiritual manner." Though this may seem like common sense, self-care is often jeopardized when you're put in difficult situations. Whether we have a challenge at work, school, family, or in-between, self-care is often put at the bottom of the to-do list. Yet, what most people fail to realize is that self-care is one of the most important things you can do for yourself and for others. Society may trick you into thinking so, but you do not, and I repeat, you do not have to be productive all the time. You lose your sense of your humanity when you prioritize productivity over your own sense of well-being. As discussed in the previous chapter, excessive productivity can cause high levels of stress leading to burnout. In addition, not engaging in a self-care routine can even lead to more challenging situations, such as suffering from depression, anxiety, resentment, and more.

THE IMPORTANCE OF SELF-CARE

Practicing self-care allows you to be more confident in all aspects of life. When you commit time to yourself, you become dedicated to being good to yourself. You are rewarding yourself and meeting needs that are unique to you. You send a positive message to your mind saying, "I matter." This is important because it's more than just putting on a face mask and calling it a day. Instead, self-care is about putting yourself in an environment that will allow you to rejuvenate and be better than the person you were yesterday.

Even mundane tasks like making time to clean your apartment, showering, washing your hair, and brushing your teeth are self-care. It's true that they're all expected of you, but they shouldn't be underestimated. When you're in a clean and orderly environment, it gives you the space to have the confidence to be the best person you can be, and this shows up in your performance. While this might be more difficult to enact, this is one of the most critical forms of self-care because if you do not allow yourself to be in a place of confidence, it'll be challenging to pursue your aspirations and to make sure you're headed in the right direction.

To go after things in life, you have to have the energy to do so. Because the truth is, you cannot do well in anything if you're always tired, have no energy, and are not in the right mindset to go after what you want. Everything you do requires you to have fuel, like an airplane preparing for a departure. If a plane doesn't have enough fuel for its flight, there's no chance it'll rise. You are the same way, and the way you recharge is through self-care.

SELF-CARE IS FOR EVERYONE

There's a common misconception that self-care consists of taking months off, going to expensive spas, and going on long vacations. While that can be incorporated into self-care every once in a while, spending a lot of money on yourself isn't necessary. The truth about self-care is that the majority of it is practical activities that not only maintain your well-being but enhance it. Lisa Butler, a professor of social work at the University of Buffalo, said in her Self-Care Starter Kit for social work students, "Originally, self-care focused around protecting or alleviating negative outcomes like stress, burnout, vicarious traumatization," she said. "But self-care is bigger than that...It's about maintaining or actually enhancing your well-being. It's going beyond manning the ramparts." Within the self-care kit, she focuses on people practicing self-care in the physical, professional, interrelation, emotional, psychological, and spiritual sense. Butler encourages people to think about which area they most want to improve within their lives. Once they figure that out, it is then time to focus on making those areas enjoyable to bring happiness to their lives.

Another fallacy that occurs concerning self-care is if you're too busy, you don't have time for self-care. In reality, the busiest people in this world need self-care just like everyone else. Below is a famous quote made by Eleanor Brown, a popular American novelist, anthologist, editor, teacher, and speaker.

"Rest and self-care are so important. When you take time to replenish your spirit, it allows you to serve others from the overflow. You cannot serve from an empty vessel."

—ELEANOR BROWN

No matter how much or how little free time you have, you always have time for self-care. In this chapter, we'll explore how to carve out time for self-care. Because if you really think it's not possible, it's now time to create this possibility through the power of Happy Meetings.

SCHEDULE HAPPY MEETINGS

When we are at work or school, we are expected to be at meetings or classes at certain times of the day. From countless calendar invites to appointments, to tasks we must complete to prepare for presentations and assignments, a schedule is laid out for you. You know what needs to get done for your classes, clients, or supervisor. However, with self-care, know that you're responsible for understanding what your needs are and when you need them. Because you might be more used to having a schedule made for you, figuring out what to schedule for your self-care needs might be challenging. Luckily, you can figure that out with Happy Meetings: meetings you make on your own terms to maintain your well-being. Inspired by Lisa Butler's Self-Care Starter Kit, Happy Meetings focus on your physical, environmental, social, and mental well-being. By taking care of your well-being in these five senses, you'll be able to give yourself the space to conquer any area of your life. As Eleanor Brown might agree, after taking these steps, your vessel will be full to serve from.

PHYSICAL HAPPY MEETINGS

Happy meetings that focus on the physical sense emphasize the importance of taking care of your physical activity and appearance. To make sure you function physically, you have to use what you have to become better, and that comes with exercise. Whether it be grinding at the gym, walking more than you drive, or even doing some yoga, physical happy meetings boost chemicals in the brain responsible for your mood. Scientists Elizabeth A. Weaver II and Hilary H. Doyle of the Dana Foundation share that when you exercise, your body releases endorphins that positively impact your mood. Throughout the exercise process, body chemicals such as dopamine and endorphins (chemicals responsible for your happiness) are produced. Simultaneously, your brain gets rid of chemicals that are responsible for stress, such as cortisol. This creates more opportunities for your brain to rewire neurons that can help you make exercise a habit.

In addition to implementing exercise as a part of a physical happy meeting, know that you need to make time to look your best as well. Making time to work on your appearance is important because it boosts your self-esteem. Doctors from Get Hair, a hair transplant company based in the United Kingdom, say, "Your self-esteem directly relates to how much you like yourself and what you think of your personal attributes and qualities. People with high self-esteem generally feel positive and confident about themselves; they believe that they have good qualities and strengths that make them valuable to society, and they also tend to be far more sociable." An important thing to remember is that when it comes to your appearance, working on it is vital to becoming comfortable in your own skin. You don't work on your appearance just because someone told you they think you're ugly. First of all, do not worry about that person because I can assure you, they're the one who's insecure. Secondly, your appearance is for you, and only for you. In order words, when you look good to yourself, you feel good.

Your appearance happy meetings should consist of times working being confident in how you look. For example, it's important that you shower on a regular basis to clean yourself and get rid of germs. But, once a week, take a longer shower where you exfoliate your skin, shave (only if you don't want hair in certain areas), and moisturize your skin. In addition, having a good skincare routine allows you to have healthier-looking skin. Using face masks on a weekly basis is a good idea too. Don't forget that scheduling time to do your hair, whether you go to the salon or barber, or do it yourself, is also huge. With appearance happy meetings, you get to take your already naturally beautiful appearance and enhance it through self-care. Know that you shouldn't feel obligated to drastically change your appearance in any way. Instead, focus on cleanliness and comfort.

ENVIRONMENTAL HAPPY MEETINGS
While physical happy meetings focus on how you present yourself, environmental happy meetings allow you to take control of your environment. To be more specific, your home is where you need to invest the most time for environmental

happy meetings, as this is the place where you're supposed to wind down after a long day of work or school. This is especially important if you must work from home.

For environmental happy meetings, make the commitment to clean parts of your home for a few minutes each day or two to three hours each week. Researchers from Princeton University concluded the more clutter that's in a person's vicinity, the more difficult it is to focus and finish tasks. Having a mess can cause you to be irritated and anxious, but by cleaning your messes consistently, you gain control of your environment by creating a space that helps you rejuvenate and focus more.

This can be easier to do if you live with a roommate, romantic partner, or family members, especially if you find cleaning to be a daunting task. Create a plan with them on how you can each tackle cleaning the spaces you all share. Just like I mentioned in Chapter 6 "Ask for Help," giving yourself the approval to depend on others gives you the opportunity to improve on your relationships with other people. As a result, you'll be less stressed and won't be overwhelmed with tasks.

SOCIAL HAPPY MEETINGS

Social happy meetings are not only one of my favorite ways to engage in self-care but are also important because it reminds us all of the fact that you aren't expected to thrive in your life alone. Regardless if you are an introvert or extrovert, connecting with people allows you to see that you are not alone. It's nice to be a part of a community that's larger than yourself. Social happy meetings not only give you the opportunity to interact with people you care about, such as your friends and family, but it also gives you the freedom to do stress-relieving activities where you invite people do self-care with you. The best thing about it is that social happy meetings can be just about anything. Getting a bite to eat, going to a fun class, sending a text to check up on a friend you miss dearly, you name it.

Even though I mentioned how everyone needs social happy meetings, some may need more than others. If you're an introvert, you might go for a week without scheduling a social happy meeting. If you're an extrovert, you probably can't go without social happy meetings more than once a week. No matter how little or how much you think you need social happy meetings, as long as you fit social happy meetings into your schedule, that's all that matters.

MENTAL HAPPY MEETINGS

Taking care of yourself mentally requires you to fuel your brain with things that make you feel good. To deal with any challenge, you have to make sure you are doing okay mentally. You can do this in many different ways, such as diving into a good book, journaling, meditating, or taking a walk outside to connect with nature. One of the most important mental happy meetings you can have is being honest with yourself about how you're doing. Don't tell yourself, "Oh, I'm fine," when you know you aren't. If you are constantly anxious, unhappy, or have difficulty identifying your feelings, then you may want to talk to a therapist about how you're doing.

Lori Gottlieb, a psychotherapist, and author of *Maybe You Should Talk to Someone*, said, "We feel like there's a hierarchy of pain, and if our problem doesn't feel big enough, we wait until we're basically having the equivalent of an emotional heart attack before somebody will make that call." One of the reasons why this may happen is the internal fear of being stigmatized for seeking treatment. Family, friends, and society impact your attitude on seeking therapy. So if you think therapy is for people who have something terribly wrong with them, reframe the way you think about mental health and schedule a session with a therapist.

I started going to therapy in 2020 with preconceived notions about mental health. After using the online service called Better Help for almost a year, here is what I learned:

- Having a therapist for your mental health is like having a personal trainer at the gym. You improve your mental health by having guidance on reaching your mental goals.
- All of your feelings, no matter what they are, are valid, especially with negative emotions. Nothing is wrong with you for not being happy all the time. In fact, you're not supposed to be happy all the time. Feel your feelings. Let yourself be sad about events that happened years ago. Let yourself celebrate the joy, even if no one else is being joyful with you.
- You are not responsible for your trauma, but you have to hold yourself accountable for your healing. People will hurt you. Whether it's strangers, exes, friends, or even your own family, the biggest revenge is to not

hurt them back. The biggest revenge is living your life in the most authentic way possible.

SELF-CARE IN THE VIRTUAL WORLD

You may see a lot of reports on how damaging the online world can be and warnings to stay away from it. But, let's be real, it's 2021. It's very difficult to avoid being in virtual spaces unless you're a monk or live on an isolated island far away from other humans. Many schools and jobs had to transition to virtual environments due to COVID-19, and the virtual world is where we get a lot of news, entertainment, and if you're like me, groceries delivered to your front door. While we do need to be careful about the dangers of the web, know that you can take control of the virtual spaces you visit frequently. By being intentional with the amount of time you're online, as well as what you do in virtual spaces, you take control of your virtual self-care.

CLEAN OUT YOUR SOCIAL MEDIA

If you have accounts on social media platforms such as Facebook, Twitter, Instagram, Snapchat, TikTok, or even LinkedIn, understand that you're responsible for the content that appears on your feed, not the people you follow. This is because when you use your social media accounts, no one is forcing you to follow anybody, and everyone has different values that may or may not align with your own. You make the decision to follow people, so you need to follow people and pages that make you feel good and closely align with your values. Therefore, one of the mental happy meetings you can schedule is time to check who you follow on social media at least once a month. You should follow people who inspire you with their content.

Examples include, but are not limited to: motivational speakers, educators, athletes, and artists. Also, you don't need to follow people just because you know them personally, especially your close friends and family. If they post stuff that displays low energy, such as excessively sharing when they get wasted or high off their ass, talking shit about people, and overall being negative, unfollow and block them. If you want to take it a step further because these posts may be a sign that you need to be concerned, check in with that person personally to see how they're doing.

Sometimes, you also need to unfollow people not because they post negative content but just to keep your own self in check. For example, let's say you're no longer friends with someone or you recently ended a romantic relationship. Regardless of whether you ended on good or bad terms with this person, you don't need to keep them on your social media, even if their posts are harmless. In real life, when you stop seeing people consistently, you learn to move on with your life without their presence. But having these people on social media makes it harder to do because while you're trying to move on, your brain is still accustomed to seeing them. That's why you might have the urge to stalk your ex's pages or check in with that friend you stopped being friends with a long time ago. The truth is, having them on social media is a waste of time because it prevents you from being in the present and looking forward to the future. Instead, it entraps you to excessively think about your past, which in the long run, stunts your growth.

Lastly, social media can be used to inform people about the social injustices of our society. While these issues are difficult to talk about, many people post about what's going on in different parts of the world to initiate action. Whether it's discussing inequality issues, wars, political challenges, or more, know it is important to know what's going on around you and understand all perspectives, including the ones you may not agree with. However, if you see too much content about the issues of the world to the point where you see your mental health decline, know it's okay to take time off the grid, especially if you feel the impact of these issues in your real life. If you are able and willing, I encourage you to help people who are suffering from social injustice. Still, it's important to understand that one person cannot solve world issues overnight. When you're getting extremely frustrated with social issues, schedule a mental happy meeting by unplugging from the digital world and plugging into nature. Maybe hang out at the park for thirty minutes or even go camping.

CLEAN OUT YOUR EMAIL

In addition to being responsible for who you follow on your social media, know that you are also responsible for your email. Emails can easily pile up like Jenga pieces. And as a result, it gets messy very quickly. Emails can be mixed with personal messages, subscriptions, newsletters, spam, and work mail. Just in 2020 alone, approximately 306 billion emails were sent worldwide on a daily basis, but only less than half of those emails were opened. By 2025, it is expected that around 376 billion emails will be sent each day. Just like it's important to keep your physical environment clean, it's also important to keep your email clean and only allow messages you really need to lower your stress.

This is important because we are communicating digitally more than previous generations. Focus and prioritize messages that matter most to you. Think of your email like the literal mailbox for your home. If you're getting thousands of letters sent to your house each day, you're going to be overwhelmed with the amounts of mail arriving at your doorstep. The solution to this would be to clean out your mail subscription, you must do the same when it comes to your email as well.

A large chunk of emails sent out is from retail companies sending promotions to their customers. One of the reasons why many people have difficulty practicing self-care is because of the common misconception that self-care is buying things in order to "treat yo-self." One of the reasons why is because of online stores and their email subscriptions, which have increased by 145 percent in 2020 alone. While "retail therapy" on an occasional basis is okay, you don't need to spend a lot of money to treat yourself.

Many businesses send out emails to their customers on what deals they have going on so they can boost their sales. When you shop online, you automatically get pop-up emails to enter your email for "50% off," "Buy One, Get One, free," and such. You don't need to subscribe to every online store just to get deals. Over time, the more stores that have your email, the more cluttered your email is going to be. As a result, when you are looking for important emails, like a recruiter trying to contact you for a job interview, you'll have a harder time getting to them.

Make a happy meeting to clean out your email by unsubscribing from email lists that do not interest you, setting your email to delete messages after a certain number of days, and being selective about which email lists you subscribe to. Just like no one is forcing you to follow anyone on social media, no one is forcing you to subscribe to all of these email lists either, even if you've been tempted with coupon codes.

BUSY PEOPLE NEED SELF-CARE TOO

I don't care how busy you are. You need self-care just like everyone else. Again, similar to the words of Eleanor Brown, you can't pour from an empty cup. Meaning, you can't be so productive for your job, school, and other responsibilities you don't make time to take care of yourself. Self-care as a busy person may seem impossible, but I promise you it's not. Sometimes self-care can only take a few minutes per day. On other days, you might need more than one hour. If you think you need quite some time to invest in your self-care, don't be afraid to ask for help, as we've discussed recently.

One of the best ways to do this is by delegating tasks to other people when needed. For example, in my sorority, I am responsible for social media marketing for my chapter. My *Hermanas* (sorority sisters), know I'm one of the busiest people on our university's campus since I'm involved in a lot of organizations, am a full-time student, have a job, and run a business.

One Friday while walking to class, I noticed I felt very sluggish, I had a huge headache, and my vision was blurry. During classes that day, I fell asleep a few times, all because I had pulled an all-nighter to work on a difficult research paper for one of my professors. After noticing I wasn't feeling my best, I asked my chapter if they could post the social media content I planned because I wanted to head back to my dorm to catch up on sleep. After they said yes, I sent them the content I planned on posting and went to my dorm to catch up on sleep for the weekend.

Ideally, you should ask for help before you sacrifice your needs. I shouldn't have pulled an all-nighter in the first place. However, I didn't share a perfect example because I want you to learn from my mistake and not neglect sleep like I did. Try to ask for help before shit hits the fan. Also, when you do ask for help, let go of the urge to have control. If you ask for someone to do you a favor, accept the fact they might do it differently than you would have.

On that day, I learned to reevaluate my priorities as a busy person. A big thing in society today, especially in the United States, is glorifying toxic productivity. I needed to unlearn notorious slogans like #workhardplayhard, and "sleep when you're dead." Since that day, I let go of commitments that don't serve me well, such as certain clubs on campus. I also learned I need to put myself first above everything else.

For all of my busy people out there, the most important thing you need to know about fitting self-care into your schedule is that communication is key. Whether it's your parents, romantic partner, kids, or friends, by communicating in advance to whoever you must inform about your need for self-care, you can work with them on whatever arrangements necessary to get your self-care in. When you emphasize your need for self-care to the people who care about you, they'll work with you however they can to make that happen. But, understand that you need to communicate these things in advance, because like yourself, people have schedules, and other people need to make time for self-care as well. In other words, they too, need to put their oxygen masks on first before helping others like yourself.

LITTLE EFFORT, BIG IMPACT

The time you need for self-care varies based on what your needs are each week. Because there are so many ways to practice self-care, make time each week to evaluate how you're going to implement it. Ideally, you should do at least a few things that pertain to self-care each week. It all depends on what you really need at the moment. Do you need to talk about something that's bothering you? Do you need to get rid of negative energy? Do you need to get your hair done? Do you need to clean your room? Plan accordingly.

CALL TO ACTION

Self-care is not a luxury. It's a necessity. For any challenge you have to overcome, you have to be confident in your abilities. If you do not invest in yourself, overcoming your challenges won't be possible, no matter how big or small.

TO-DO LIST

- Think of five things you want to do for happy meetings.
- Schedule your five happy meetings over the course of five weeks or less.
- After you finish your happy meeting, reflect on your experience and how that meeting made you feel.
- Clean out your social media and email.

PART IV

BEGIN TO RISE

9

TURN GOALS INTO ACHIEVEMENTS

———

"Picture yourself in your mind's eye as having already achieved this goal. See yourself doing the things you'll be doing when you've reached your goal."

—EARL NIGHTINGALE

Have you ever had a group chat with your friends and tried to make plans to see each other? Although there are a lot of things to do, the conversation usually starts like this:

Friend A: *"What do u want to do?"*

Friend B: *"Idk what do u want to do?*

Friend C: *"Let's check out this new restaurant."*

Friend D: *"Let's stay in."*

Friend A: *"I'm not hungry."*

And then the conversation goes on for an hour about what y'all are trying to do. Then the next thing you know, you end up just meeting up that evening, looking for the restaurant Friend C suggested, then arrive and realize the restaurant is closed for the night! Then you're back at square one, trying to see what y'all are trying to do. Before you know it, you've used up a lot of your time together just figuring out what the plan is.

If you aren't committed to where you want to go, it will be difficult to get anywhere, which is especially important with your goals. It is very easy to think of goals. Whether you want to create multiple streams of income, land a record deal, or lose weight. You can say a whole bunch of things to yourself. You can have inspirational quotes on your wall, read a lot of books such as this one for motivation, and dream all you want. While being driven is important, your goals can easily turn into a pile of garbage if you aren't actively putting in the work to turn them into reality. To turn your goals into achievements, you are required to create consistent actions that direct you on the right path.

To do this, you have to understand who you are. When you understand who you are, you can know your why. When you know your why, you're able to use that as fuel to power you through action. When you fail, your why is always going to be there to remind you to get back up. Therefore, when it comes to turning your goals into achievements, you have to pursue a powerful purpose, be consistently consistent, and learn to rise after you fall.

PURSUE A POWERFUL PURPOSE

Purpose is defined as "the reason for which something exists or is done, made, used, etc." In other words, your purpose is the why. If you are currently stuck, it's because you lack momentum. You're still. Your purpose is not what you're told to do. Rather, it's what you want to do. It's not your parents telling you what to do. It's not your friends or your significant other telling you what's best for you. Your purpose enables you to find what exactly you want to do in your life. To find it, you have to understand who you truly are. As mentioned in Part 1, you have to appreciate where you've been to appreciate where you'll be. When you understand who you truly are and where you have been, you will discover your why. A meaningful purpose demonstrates powerful emotion. It's what wakes you up in the morning and what makes you go to sleep at night ready for the next day.

Dr. Alan R. Zimmerman, author of *The Payoff Principle,* said, "When you find purpose in what you do, exhibit passion for the outcome, and master the process to make it happen, you produce the payoffs you want, need, and deserve in every domain of your life." In addition, he writes in his book that a purpose sits on a three-legged stool. The three legs represent the following questions. One: What difference do you want to make? Two: What are you good at? Three: What excites you? These three questions are essential for you to answer if you want to know your purpose for achieving your specific goal. If you do not have the answer to all three, your purpose will not be supported by the three-legged stool. There will be no equilibrium to place your purpose upon.

For you to make sure you understand your why, you need some inspiration. To have some inspiration, you need a mission statement. Think of your favorite companies. Whether it's Nike, Tesla, or Starbucks, google your favorite company's mission statement. For Nike, their mission is "To bring inspiration and innovation to every athlete in the world." For Tesla, their mission statement is "To accelerate the world's transition to sustainable energy." For Starbucks, their mission statement is "To inspire and nurture the human spirit – one person, one cup, and one neighborhood at a time."

You need to have a mission statement because it brings your why to life. It guides you to how you'll approach your process and how your passion will be fueled. What I love about mission statements is that they can be as short or as long as you want. Not one mission statement should be like anyone else's because it is supposed to be unique to that person or individual. While it is okay to have similar goals and interests, your mission statement should be unique to you. My mission statement, for example, is "To instill purpose in communities through meaningful innovation." While this may be simple, it holds a lot of weight to me for several reasons. First, my very own name, Nia, is derived from Swahili, meaning "purpose." Within my mission statement, I wanted to make it very clear that my why was to help other people find their "why." Second, a mission statement serves to explain how you will specifically help the world. For me, my world involves the communities that made me the person I am today. Lastly, it explains my how. As a creative individual, meaningful innovation describes how I will solve problems for my community in the best way I know how, and that is being creative. Throughout this book, I've shared stories of my appreciation for art and its power on a larger scale. Also, I am helping others find their "why" through writing my book. When you create your mission statement, it does not have to be long. What matters is that you create a mission statement that aligns with what you would like to pursue.

To understand your purpose, write a mission statement, or even utilize the three-legged stool, you must understand your why. Your why is your reason for being, your reason for giving, and your reason to be on this Earth. To figure out your purpose, you must find what excites you and how that excitement will make a difference in this world. Finding your purpose consists of discovering what's most important to you. This is something that may not happen overnight. However, you must recognize that there's a lot you can do to figure this out. In addition to self-reflection, aspects of purpose, such as writing the mission statement, think about trying things you've always wanted to try. Ask yourself, how did this action make me feel? A great way to do this is through volunteering. Try experimenting with different community organizations. Focus on something that is of interest to you. Not only will you be serving your community, but you can utilize that experience later on in your life, such as applying for a job, internship, or school.

Don't just sign up for any volunteer event. Find an organization or volunteer event of interest to you. Whether you're interested in the arts, culture, or sports, there are so many volunteer opportunities available. You can find them by googling or asking your friends and family if they know of opportunities. Even your faith-based community, such as your church or mosque, will have something for you. Think about what is of interest to you. Grab a notebook and a pen and write down seven to ten things that are of interest to you that you haven't tried. That is your starting point.

LET YOUR PURPOSE WRITE YOUR GOALS

When you think of constructing a building, many steps are involved. You need a foundation to support the building, otherwise it will sink. You need to plan what you're constructing and ensure you're using the right materials to build the building. Lastly, every day you need to keep on building until your construction is complete. Your purpose is like the foundation for a construction project. Whether it's a house or a skyscraper, the foundation is what the entire project rests on. When you have your foundation right, you'll be able to construct the building without complications. The construction materials, as you may have guessed, are your goals. Your goals need to be supported by your purpose. Otherwise, the project will fail.

Once you have your purpose down, as discussed previously in this chapter, take time to ensure your goals align with your purpose. Again, your purpose is the "why," so your goals are the "how" you're going to pursue your "why." Let's go back to the company mission statements listed above, specifically Starbucks's mission statement. Their mission statement is, "To inspire and nurture the human spirit – one person, one cup, and one neighborhood at a time." With this mission statement, it's safe to say one of their goals is to make coffee people enjoy.

That goal isn't hard to create because when you read their mission statement, it creates a foundation for their goals. Think about the relationship between your goals and your mission statement like the process of constructing a building.

"When we build, let us think that we build forever."

—JOHN RUSKIN

A strong foundation is essential to the longevity of your final building. If a foundation can't support what you intend to build, everything will fall apart. So when you create your goals, make sure all of your goals align with your mission statement. If your goals do not align with your mission statement, you won't be able to achieve your goals since your purpose won't support it.

BE CONSISTENTLY CONSISTENT

To turn your goals into accomplishments, read the following line in your mind. Then, read it out loud, and then write it down in your notebook.

To turn your goals into achievements, be consistently consistent by overcoming inconsistency.

The only way to learn how to do a push-up the right way is to do a push-up.

You're going to do it wrong when you do it the first time. When your PE teacher said for you and all the other students to do a push-up in your first PE class in school, I'm sure you fucked up. I did too, but eventually, after continuing to practice your push-up in PE class and even at home, if you're ambitious, you're going to get better.

When you have a strong purpose and goals that align with this purpose, the next step is to be willing to work at your goals by creating consistent actions that help you get there. The willingness to do things, again and again, allows you to do things better. You won't get better overnight, and this idea is not new. This applies to everything you want to get better at, from earning an A in your calculus class, to becoming the top salesperson at work, to overall becoming a better person.

With 365 days in a year, there are 365 chances to improve yourself, but that comes with the power of consistency. To explain this better, look at the equation below:

$$(1.00)^{365} = 1.00$$

The 1.00 represents you every day. With 365 days in a year, if you do not do anything at all to improve yourself, you will be stagnant at the end of the year and not see any growth. But look at this next equation:

$$(1.01)^{365} = 37.7$$

The 0.01 added to your (1.00) represents you and the small, consistent efforts you put in each day to work on the goals you made for yourself. As a result, 1.01 to the 365th power results in 37.7, a higher value than 1.00 to the 365th power. Small but consistent efforts each day throughout the year will give you larger results by the end of the year than staying stagnant. You don't want to be stuck at a 1.00. When you allow yourself to be consistent, even if the efforts are small, in the long-term, you will have a better result compared to not doing anything at all.

To be consistently consistent, you have to make sure you allow yourself to avoid inconsistency. You become consistent when you allow yourself to let priorities control your time, make good habits, and understand the components of change.

PRIORITIES CONTROL YOUR TIME

One day consists of 86,400 seconds, and it's important that you utilize each second to get yourself closer to achieving your goals. Each action you take each day should be aligned with your goals. In doing so, you give yourself the ability to come closer and closer to your goal. The problem that arises, however, is that with all these seconds in a day, it's easy to get distracted by the limitless amounts of options you have as to how to spend your time.

To ensure your time isn't wasted each day, you need to change your mindset on choices. Life choices can be like a lot of options at a buffet. You don't eat everything off the menu at a buffet. Most people pick about five things to eat and then return to their table. You can't take in anything more once you're full. Therefore, you need to make choices that only align with your purpose and goals. These specific choices you make are your priorities, and these are responsible for controlling your time. This process eliminates all the unnecessary choices that steer you away from your goal. This idea is explained in Cranfield and Hansen's *The New York Times* best-seller *Chicken Soup for the Soul*. They created and practiced the rule of five based on advice from their school teacher, who shared the analogy of a lumberjack cutting down a tree:

"If you go every day to a very large tree and take five swings at it with a very sharp axe, eventually, no matter how large the tree, it would have to come down."

Throughout the process of writing my book, I committed to five actions to ensure I would get this book published. Here is what I did consistently throughout this process:

1. Wrote down on a Post-it Note "Your book is already here. You just need to write it," and stuck it to my wall.
2. Meditated for a minimum of five minutes.
3. Researched how people overcome their challenges.
4. Outlined my thoughts into tangible chapter outlines.
5. Wrote and revised my chapters.

While this was never done in the same order each day, these actions explained how I achieved my goal of writing a book. My goal of writing my book aligns with my purpose of helping others instill the power of purpose in their own lives. The rule of five eliminates the buffet of choices and narrows down the actions you need to take to get closer to your goal, as your goals are your priorities.

DEVELOP GOOD HABITS AND KEEP THEM

Throughout the process of executing your goals, you need to understand the importance of creating habits. Habits are small actions you take each day to get closer to your goal. Ish Verduzco, author of *Get Ish Done*, said in his book, "Make your habit easy." Habits are a part of the process of achieving your goals. So while they should be easy, it is essential they have a purpose and that they fuel your passion for creating habits that will stick. Not only do your habits have to be easy, but the habits also need to be rewarding in the long run. For example, if you decide to make working out a consistent habit, you can reward yourself with a sweet every few weeks. Or, if you make it a habit to put money away in a savings account, make sure to save money aside for a nice vacation each year.

Block off time where you could be putting your passion and energy toward your goal. Don't get me wrong, I sleep in on the weekends, and sometimes I like to play games on my phone. However, be sure you're not overdoing it with sleeping in or other bad habits that take away from your time achieving that goal. Ish Verduzco also explains that sacrifices give your good habits the power because good habits require sacrifices. He writes in his book, "It's in the sacrifice that a habit can become empowering and transform into a ritual."

Everything you desire will cost you one of the following: time, energy, or money.

In several cases, your desires may cost all three, especially if you desire to start a business one day. Nevertheless, take into consideration what you're willing to sacrifice to reach your goal. Without sacrifice, there is no habit. This goes both ways. When you sleep in, you sacrifice time in which you can be working on your goal. When you don't sleep enough, you sacrifice energy that could propel you into making progress with your goal. So when you create habits, make sure you're making sacrifices that are worthwhile. In other words, do not sacrifice your health for the sake of achieving your goal. As mentioned in Chapter 8 "Practice Self-Care," you want to make sure you can enjoy the results of the work you put in.

UNDERSTAND THE COMPONENTS OF CHANGE

To turn goals into achievements, you need to make habits that have a sacrifice, and that sacrifice requires you to change. A lot of times, people are afraid to change because our brains are wired to stay in our comfort zone. When you try something different for the first time, your brain will want to back out because it's uncomfortable. On top of that, society has common misconceptions about change, such as how it takes time, how you have to want change, and changes can only occur when something really drastic has happened to a person. However, Andy Andrews, *New York Times* best-selling author, has debunked these myths. He states, "These myths are obliterated, when two things are clearly made clear. One, the person who needs to change, understands what's in it for them. Two, the person has proved beyond a reasonable doubt that they should change."

Having a good understanding of what's in it for you and having enough self-awareness to realize you should change, will drive everything else in terms of your passion. Your purpose, process, and your habit-building upon this self-discovery, mixed with activities designed to help you reach your goal, will take you in the right direction of executing your goals. One way to keep yourself accountable is by documenting the experience. So, you should use the same notebook you used to write your mission statement to confirm your process of executing your goals each day moving forward.

Create a journal of what you do each day to get yourself closer to your goal. From the very beginning, you're going to find some challenges. Some days may be easier than others or some days may be harder than others, but what is essential is figuring out what goals you want to achieve. You keep on executing your plans on a daily basis. You must create a habit to keep on working toward your goals each day. Creating a journal keeps you accountable internally so you can reflect on the process you've created for yourself. This change will allow you to see what works well and what doesn't. As a result, you will not only have a record of your behaviors, but in the future, you'll understand what you need to do to get yourself to the right place.

RISE UP AFTER YOU FALL

For any goal that you set, understand that failure is inevitable. No matter your skill level, there is never a guarantee that you'll succeed. So when you fail at your goals, you must accept what's happened. Everyone fails, but what allows people to succeed is making the decision to get up after they've been knocked down. You have to accept the fact that failures happen.

In the book, *The Hidden Power of F*cking Up* by The Try Guys, they write:

> *"Failure is a step forward, not a step back. It's helpful to remember that some of the greatest writers, thinkers,*

athletes, and musicians of our day are not special in any way whatsoever, except that they learned how to fail and get back up again. No one is born great. Have you seen babies? They can't even hold pencils, those dummies. Greatness isn't something ordained—it's something you work your ass off for, despite failing over and over again."

Failure is a sign that you've tried. In the process of trying, you're learning lessons that will be of value to you when you try to achieve your goals the next time around. When you fail, you give yourself experience. Experience gives you wisdom. Wisdom gives you lessons. So by the time you're ready to go for your goals again, you'll have more knowledge that'll propel you to achievement.

CALL TO ACTION

To properly execute your goals, it's important to recognize your desires. Turning desires into reality require you to sacrifice your temporary desires for your long-term ones. This will not only allow for you to apply the payoff principle but to actually see your goals come from your notebook into real life. By making your habits simple and working toward your habits every day, it will lead you closer to your goal. Throughout the process of executing your goals, you'll notice yourself changing in a good way and learn to identify what changes have to occur to accomplish future goals. You'll also learn to appreciate the journey. At the end of the day, don't be so lost in working toward your goal that you forget to appreciate the journey. This will allow you to not only head in the right direction but also allow you to become more self-aware and grow overall.

TO-DO LIST

- Write your mission statement.
- Write down your goals.
- Take five actions each day that help you reach your goals.
- Allow yourself to breathe when you fail.

10

NEVER STOP LEARNING

——

Six thousand is the number of thoughts the average person has in a single day.

A person has thoughts about food, what's going on in their current situation, and odd peripheral thoughts too. Our minds are always thinking about something. And within those moments, our minds impact our decision-making. Our brains are always thinking about more things to think about. It's always on the search for more.

In addition to random thoughts, our brains think a lot about what we already know. Whether that be our minds thinking about what we learned from one of our teachers, what we learned from a TEDx Talk, or even through a conversation we've had with one of our friends. Our minds get bored very quickly, and so we turn to our phones to scroll through social media, watch entertaining videos, and allow ourselves to fill the void by watching an illusion. Our favorite traveling pages make us believe we're halfway across the world when we're just lying down in bed. In our search for satisfaction with social media, we think we are satisfied. You might convince yourself you're in Tahiti because you just saw your Instagram feed, but you're still in bed; you're still in the same spot. That fulfillment you thought you had scrolling through Instagram is now gone. You've lost both your time and your energy. There's no commitment involved in an action when there's little to no work required. However, the more you commit yourself to things, the more satisfied you'll become for extended periods. Prolonged satisfaction is meaningful when we make it a mission to learn, and when you commit to becoming a lifelong learner, you'll become more fulfilled.

As humans, we are wired to always ask questions, even when we don't realize we have something to add. Becoming a lifelong learner allows you to learn more about yourself and the rest of the world. Do you think we automatically knew why the sky was blue? Do you think we created vaccines as an attempt to end the COVID-19 pandemic just overnight? The biggest challenges, questions, and ideas all come to light when we take it upon ourselves to become lifelong learners. Therefore, as people, we get so fascinated with witty, fun facts. The process of becoming better requires us to be better. How do we do that?

Get comfortable with the uncomfortable by never ending your learning journey. By utilizing the resources around us and seeking new knowledge, we grow our biggest superpower that allows us to be the best person we can be. But how do we get there? What allows us to become lifelong learners? It's not as difficult as you think because you have access to everything at your fingertips, thanks to the power of the internet. To become a lifelong learner, you have to get in the habit of exposing yourself to more new things and develop a growth mindset.

SKILL DEGRADATION IS REAL

A few months after this book is published, I will graduate from High Point University with a degree in international business and a Spanish minor. Then, I will be automatically set for life. Because, you know, I'm done! Right?

Wrong, having a degree does not mean you have it all. This might sound scary but living in the modern age is a big advantage. It's a lot easier for a person to become a better learner nowadays because you're encouraged to not only rely on traditional learning environments such as school but to create a better you by having multiple perspectives from different learning mediums. This will enhance the way you think. We're in a world that forces us to learn continuously outside of the traditional school system. Digital innovator, serial entrepreneur, author, and speaker, Nikki Barua explained in her podcast *Beyond Barriers,* that skills now become "obsolete" in eighteen months or less on account of rapid changes in technology. As a result, 50 percent of employees worldwide will have to be re-skilled just to stay competitive. "Essentially, everyone has to redo everything," she said.

Becoming a lifelong learner is not only enjoyable, but it can save you. Once you graduate from your final educational institution, it's very easy to have this mindset where you say, "Okay, that's it. I'm done." But that is not the case. Although the pressure of getting good grades in school can take a toll on you, you cannot allow yourself to stop learning after graduation. Your problems don't end after you throw your cap in the sky. So why treat learning that way?

YOU WILL BE HAPPIER

Being in a world of instant gratification makes us slaves to the web. We have Siri and Alexa to answer all of our questions. Google can show you the world without making you leave your house. It sounds like a chore to want to learn for fun. Yet, what allows for the smiles on our faces are those "I did it" moments, the moments where you figure something out. Those moments when you look like a cartoon character with a lightbulb over their head. The moments when you say, "Hmm... that's interesting. I didn't know that." These moments are what Hungarian American psychologist Mihaly Csikszentmihalyi calls our "state of flow." His theory states that when we're very invested in learning about something, nothing else matters at that moment. And to enter into the flow, we must be challenged by something that intrigues us.

This is what keeps your brain active. This is why our brains have those several thousand thoughts and strive to have more. We must commit ourselves to learning because when we invest in our knowledge, we invest in ourselves and who we wish to become. To invest in ourselves, we do not need to just rely on formal education. We can utilize various resources outside of traditional school to work for ourselves. People post valuable content on the internet to learn from, allowing the opportunity to enhance your learning with the traditional school environment you participate in. Just with this alone, we already have more options compared to those before us.

What is it about leaders like George Washington Carver and Katherine Johnson? How was it they all accomplished amazing things? It wasn't that they spent all-nighters on something or wanted to be someone. They all have something in common. They were all great at what they did. It wasn't because they were so set on being the best. Rather, regardless of their situation, they never stopped learning. The people who are most successful in this world never stop learning. And why would they? It sets you up for life. For every challenge you face, a solution will always be discovered after you learn something new. Being committed to lifelong learning allows you to do well because you're always moving forward. Being stagnant won't get you anywhere and trying to limit yourself is boring and dangerous.

THE POWER OF GROWTH MINDSET

Allowing yourself to become a lifelong learner enables you to have a growth mindset. A growth mindset is the belief that with consistent efforts and willingness to learn, you can improve your current abilities. In one study conducted by the National Library of Medicine, researchers experimented with math students who completed a program about how intellectual abilities improved with growth and development. Compared with the math students who did not complete the program, the students who did learn about the power of growth mindset had overall higher averages in their test scores.

Being able to have a growth mindset allows you to become comfortable with lifelong learning because you accept the fact that learning requires challenges along the way. Many people see challenges as a roadblock. However, when you think of challenges as an opportunity, you give yourself the space to grow and develop as a human being.

CALL TO ACTION

While Hasan Minhaj was a student at the University of California in Davis, he studied political science and was a great student. But when he wasn't in class or working on assignments, he was investing his time into learning about something he really liked, and that was comedy.

The first stand-up special he watched was Chris Rock's *Never Scared*. From then on, Hasan was hooked. Hasan began reading books on comedy and watched more comedy specials. It got to the point where he was no longer watching greats like Chris Rock or Eddie Murphy just to get a good laugh. He began watching their comedy specials to study them. The more he watched, the more he learned. Hasan began writing his own material, and soon after, he started performing out of comedy clubs in San Francisco. Because he was consistent in perfecting his craft, he began to land himself more opportunities. From performing in more cities across California, to eventually perform on NBC's Stand-up for Diversity, Hasan knew he loved comedy, and he was willing to do anything and everything to perfect his craft. As a result of learning comedy skills in his own time, Hasan had the opportunity to gain even more opportunities, such as having his own show on Netflix.

Create a list of things you'd love to learn more about. Then grab a book and read about it, whether it's a book about learning how to fly a plane, making art, dancing, coding, or even politics. Every week you should grab a book about something you'd love to learn. (Here's a hint: You're getting a great head start by reading this book about self-development.)

Secondly, listen to a good podcast with apps like Spotify, NPR, and Apple Music; people make valuable content about just about anything, from podcasts about Wall Street to learning how to identify a serial killer who may or may not be lurking in your presence. Whatever you're interested in, know there's a podcast made especially for you. Not only are we living in a time of plentiful resources right beneath our fingertips with the power of the internet, but we're also able to learn in multiple ways. You don't need to have a college degree to be knowledgeable about something. Yes, having a degree can help you become more educated and give you more credibility. But even if you can't get a college degree, this doesn't mean you'll never be able to learn a thing. Being able to learn your way gives you more flexibility. It allows you to become more well-rounded.

Lastly, committing to lifelong learning allows you to give yourself the freedom to teach yourself something new and to teach others. When you have the chance to learn about something new from a podcast, book, or research, people will love to learn about what you've learned. Don't believe me? Take a look at the podcasts you see and the books you've read. They always give credit to the people they've learned from. The most successful people do not stagnate. Rather, they wonder why things happen and why things are the way that they are. They take everything they have and utilize it to find a solution. The next successful person to ever roam the Earth is you. Starting now, think of a topic you'd love to learn about. Guess what you should do next? Go learn about it.

11

NEVER RUN AWAY FROM CHALLENGES

---

*"I don't run away from a challenge because
I am afraid. Instead, I run toward it
because the only way to escape fear is
to trample it beneath your feet."*

—NADIA COMANECI

On July 4, 1952, Florence May Chadwick was on her way to becoming the first woman to attempt the twenty-six-mile swim between the California coastline and Catalina Island. For the duration of the long-distance swim, Chadwick traveled with a boat team who would warn her of the presence of sharks and to be prepared for unexpected injuries. Her arms circled forward with her fingertips leading the way. She was striving to reach the shore, but every time she looked through her goggles, all she could see was the dense fog.

The fog was so dense she could hardly even see the support boats following her. The ocean was cold, the waters were deep, and the grease that helped warm her in the water began to wear off. Her mother happened to be in one of the boats and gave her the encouragement to keep going after the fifteen-hour mark. Unable to see the shore, Florence Chadwick gave up after hour sixteen. She headed back to the California coastline on a boat with her team.

After Chadwick got back on the boat, she was informed that she was less than one mile away from the finish line. Had she known she was so close to the end of the swim, she could have pushed through to the end of the journey. The cold waters wouldn't have bothered her nor the jellyfish nearby. Just the year before, she was the first woman to swim from England to France and back. And for this long-distance swim in California, what pushed her back was unfavorable conditions.

This challenge was something the swimmer was prepared to face. Having done numerous long-distance swims in the past, the only difference between this race and the others was that Chadwick couldn't see the coastline. Due to the lack of perspective, she kept on saying to herself, "I can't. I can't," when in fact, she could have.

For the next two months, Florence May Chadwick went back to training. She knew if she only had seen the island, she would have finished the endurance swim. When she returned to try the swim for the second time, she had her goal in her mind. Not only did she finish the swim this time around, but she surpassed the men's long-distance speed record by two hours.

Starting something new is supposed to scare you. Regardless if you're just starting or less than half a mile away from completing your goal, it's imperative you never run away from your challenges. It's very easy to run away from your problems because of the adrenaline rush that kicks in. But eventually, that sensation goes away. You still have the issue lying in front of you. As a result, you want to find ways to hurt other people through your source of trouble. However, now is the time you learn to control these harmful behaviors to live a life worth living. By learning how to face your challenges head-on, you will unlock capabilities you never thought you had.

We have moments in our lives when we feel like escaping is part of the solution. Whether we want to leave someone to leave our problems behind or leave situations requiring a solution before separation, running away always sounds attractive. As people, we're naturally more inclined to desire comfortable conditions. We want to leave our past behind and be able to start over. However, the ability to escape situations that require our attention for them to be solved will jumpstart your growth every time. When we have challenges that we must face, it is crucial that we meet them head-on and not run away. However, no matter how big or small, all challenges contribute to your overall development and sense of being.

Procrastination can easily take control of the mind because it is uncomfortable with responsibilities. While it's expected we take care of our somewhat small responsibilities, we must continue to work on the challenges we face with our dreams in the front of our minds.

HELLO TO VIRTUAL REALITY

We tend to run away from our challenges because we don't have a connection with our future selves who would appreciate our resilience today. In a 2011 study conducted at Stanford University, researchers asked two groups of college undergraduate students to think about themselves today, a stranger ten years from now and themselves ten years from now. One of the groups of college undergraduates received immersive virtual reality animations of themselves ten years into the future, while the other group did not. Simultaneously, all college undergraduate students were assigned a hypothetical money task and then miscellaneous tasks to complete afterward. After the experiment concluded, the college undergraduates who saw themselves ten years into the future saved more money in their hypothetical savings account than the students who did not. The researchers who conducted this experiment had this as their primary objective: to identify how people can bond with their future selves and the relationship with their retirement savings.

The challenge of saving for retirement is an excellent example of a challenge people tend to run away from. Yet, if people do not have enough retirement savings, they will likely work long past the average age of retirement and live in poverty during their later years. The overall trend of people not having enough savings for retirement (besides the socioeconomic inequalities that may come into play) relates to people not motivated to invest in themselves for the future. Because it's unknown what we'll be like in the future, our minds allow us to believe that our future selves are strangers. We don't know our future selves and therefore aren't connected with them. We'll all eventually become our future selves, and we must prepare for that reality. Because here is the truth; all of the challenges attached to our goals, from the micro ones such as cleaning our home, to something long-term such as saving for retirement, are not for our present selves. However, persevering through your present-day challenges will be something your future self will thank you for.

So how do we face our challenges head-on and not run away? Well, we discussed in Part 1 how important it is to understand who you are in order to execute your goals properly, and that's partially the answer. If you feel you still must work on getting better at that, go back and revisit Part 1 before you come back here. Take your time. I will wait.

To face your challenges head-on requires that you understand your inner self to get ahead with your goals. I will discuss three methods. However, you can only pick one out of the first two, and you must enhance the first or second method you pick with the third one. But before I go into what each of these methods are, let me tell you a quick story.

(In the interest of preserving privacy, all names have been changed.)

I once met a girl in my university named Zoey. She was so sweet and one day invited me to her dorm on a Saturday night. That night, I knew I couldn't stay too long. I had a history paper due the next day by 11:59 p.m. The thing is, Zoey ended up roping me into a conversation with this guy named Sergio, and man did the quality of that exchange drive me to take several shots. It was evident Sergio had done some pregaming before I arrived. He kept saying too much about himself, things like, "My dad is the CEO of a hedge fund in SoCal," and "I know all of the CEOs of the Silicon Valley...I'm starting a new company with Mark Zuckerberg. I'm going to buy a big mansion with my inheritance from my dad's hedge fund..."

And it went on and on.

I literally wanted to vomit. Not only did Sergio present himself as extremely arrogant and obsessed with his dad's money, but I knew deep down everything sounded too good to be true. A few days later, I found out I was correct. Zoey told me she stopped talking to Sergio because she eventually found out he was full of shit. Not only did he never go on to do the things he said he was going to do, but he also lied about being the son of a hedge fund CEO. He even turned out to be an asshole and a liar to Zoey, even during the times he was sober. I wanted to share Sergio's story with you because we're going to use it as an example here for method one, and this method requires that you rise up quietly.

1. RISE UP QUIETLY

To rise up quietly, you'll work on your goals without anyone knowing in the very beginning. Give yourself time to accomplish something. Each day, work until you either achieve this goal or need outside assistance. Throughout this time, you'll be working on your goal and figuring out what challenges you're capable of handling yourself. That way, you're focused on utilizing your strengths to give you the momentum past the starting point, the most difficult part of starting to overcome your challenges.

This method works best if you know you want the most extraordinary life for yourself, but the people around you won't understand your ambition, especially if it's a massive goal. For example, one of my favorite mentors, Jade Darmawangsa, was only sixteen years old when she wanted to start her first business. Given that she was only in high school, many of the students around her were not starting businesses. They were focused on studying for the SATs and hanging out with their cliques after the last bell rang. While there's nothing wrong with this, it was clear to Jade that she was thinking differently than her peers and therefore couldn't get the help she needed. She researched entrepreneurship on the internet and learned what she could on her own.

After doing her own research, she made a list of fifty entrepreneurs who inspired her. From there, she sent them emails offering them free labor. In exchange for the free work, she asked for their mentorship. When it came time for her to launch her own business, not only were the people in her high school shocked and excited to support her but clients and companies wanted to support her business right away as a result of the independent research and the free work she did for the entrepreneurs. They recommended Jade to their networks because she had built trust and exhibited a hard work ethic from the very beginning.

Notice how rising up quietly is not rising up in silence. You need to give yourself time, in the beginning, to work on some challenges alone. Then you ask for assistance only from those who can help you. This way, you avoid unwanted attention that may distract you. By only keeping a few people aware of your goals, you won't feel unwanted attention by people who can't directly help you. The rise up quietly method works if you know you don't have support from your community or often let attention get to your head.

Former entrepreneur Derek Sivers shares in his TEDx Talk the idea of "social reality." He says when you tell your goal to someone else, and they acknowledge it, the mind perceives the goal as having been met. As a result of achieving the artificial status action, your mind will not want to do the work to achieve the goal and overcome its challenges simply because that early satisfaction is enough for you not to pursue your goal.

Does this sound familiar? It should, because Sergio, who we met earlier, is a prime example of someone stuck in their social reality. Because he shared too much with others in the early stages, his mind thought he was the cofounder of a company with Mark Zuckerberg, even though Mark Zuckerberg most likely has no idea who Sergio is.

In your own life, know that if you don't have people who are knowledgeable about something you want to do, don't tell all the details of your projects to them. Not everyone on the block needs to know your business. You need to make sure you're speaking to the right people about the right things. When you find the right people who can support you when you have challenges achieving your goals, they won't let you run away from your challenges when things get too difficult. But let's say you're lucky. You're surrounded by like-minded people who are knowledgeable about your interests and genuinely want to see you succeed. You have a strong network, and you know your network well enough to understand. This is where the Accountability Act comes in.

2. THE ACCOUNTABILITY ACT

The Accountability Act is a commitment you make to yourself and your community that keeps you accountable. This act requires you to tell your entire network a goal you're working on and asking your community to help keep you accountable. The Accountability Act requires you to keep on going with your goal and not run away from the challenges that come along with it. You are going to rely on your community for your support, and they do not need to be knowledgeable on the subject. As long as you keep sharing your story and they cheer you on, you're in a good spot.

This method works if you're motivated by encouragement. This is why when people want to become more fit, oftentimes, people create an accountability page on social media and post their workouts. This way, people can engage and support regardless of their location. However, for this to work, you must share your truth with others and display authenticity, even during the challenges that come along. Once you do this, you'll be encouraged by others to fight through your obstacles instead of running away from them. Along the way, you'll be inspiring others and eventually have people join your journey too.

Make sure you're humble during the entire process. Don't be like Sergio and be vain about your ambitions. Otherwise, your community won't want to follow you on your journey, and you won't have the encouragement you need to not run away from challenges.

3. APPLY THE FIVE-SECOND RULE

For every goal you must achieve, it requires you to complete tasks based on ideas. Mel Robbins, author and motivational speaker, discusses this in her book, *The Five Second Rule*. The five-second rule states the following:

> *"The moment you have an instinct on a goal, you must 5-4-3-2-1 and physically move, or your brain will stop you."*
> —MEL ROBBINS, AUTHOR OF *THE FIVE SECOND RULE*

This metacognition must be applied when you're completing your goals because a huge part of not running away from your challenges is doing the things that make you uncomfortable. Whether it be waking up earlier, sending an email you've been putting off sending, or submitting your application to that internship you've been doubting you're qualified for, the biggest challenge in your life is making your brain agree to do uncomfortable things.

DECIDE YOUR PATH

In this chapter, three methods were discussed to overcome the urge to run away from your challenges. To not run away, you must understand who you truly are to get on your path that was meant for you, whether it is one and three or two and three. Know that you must face them head-on. The way you choose to take it is dependent on who you are. No one knows yourself better than you do. And regardless of which path you take to make yourself face your challenges head-on, know that your future self will thank you for it.

You may be asking what goals you should start with. If there isn't a goal you currently have right now, start by creating a 401(k). After all, it's not the wrong place to start, considering the poverty we discussed is waiting for people who procrastinate saving. With the investment account, create a consistent amount of investments you'll contribute. By accepting the challenge to invest in your future self consistently, you will make decisions that will allow you to invest in your own future. For example, the money you use to buy a cup of coffee each morning could be money you use to put into your retirement account. If you can commit to yourself by investing in your future self, you will be facing the challenge of impulsive spending head-on. Start saving money today so you can invest in your future self. Again, your future self will thank you for it, and the fog will begin to clear.

TO-DO LIST
- Practice rising up quietly or implementing the accountability act.
- Apply the five-second rule when you feel the urge to procrastinate on a task.

12

NOTHING HAPPENS OVERNIGHT

"The key is this: Meet today's problems with today's strength. Don't start tackling tomorrow's problems until tomorrow. You do not have tomorrow's strength yet. You simply have enough for today."

—MAX LUCADO

In her village, Mabinty was called "The Devil's Child."

She was born in 1995 during the Sierra Leone Civil War. During that time, one of the few ways to bring some young girls stability was to get married. But, because Mabinty had vitiligo, a skin condition that causes a loss of skin pigment in certain areas, her village called her the Devil's Child. When her parents realized that arranging a marriage for Mabinty wasn't going to work, they knew they needed to find another solution for her future. Mabinty's father began teaching her the Arabic alphabet and stood up for her in the village when people talked about her skin. Both of her parents wanted to save as much money as they could for Mabinty so she could eventually get a formal education. Unfortunately, that plan didn't work out.

Not too long after Mabinty was born, her parents were killed by the *debils* (rebels of the Revolutionary United Front). Locals combined the word "devil" with "rebel" in her village. Her uncle became her primary caretaker, but he eventually sent her to a nearby orphanage. Unlike Mabinty's parents, her uncle also believed she was the Devil's Child, and in the orphanage, the caretakers and other children felt the same on account of how vitiligo was horribly portrayed within the country. One windy day, young Mabinty caught a floating magazine paper in her hands and tucked it away in her underwear for safekeeping. Later she found that on the page was a beautiful creature who she believed showed a surreal amount of joy and happiness. Though she was receiving the least amount of food, toys, and care in the orphanage, Mabinty knew she wanted to be like the beautiful creature on the magazine paper.

She showed the magazine cover to her English teacher in the orphanage, one of the few people she trusted. The teacher smiled and said, "That lady you see is a ballerina, which means 'little dancer.'"

"Well, one day, I will be like the lady in the magazine!" Mabinty smiled as she began to try to dance on her tippy toes around the gates of the orphanage. Before the other caretakers saw the paper, Mabinty hid it in her underwear again because there was nowhere else to hide it.

Mabinty and another girl in the orphanage eventually got adopted by two loving parents from the United States. Mabinty became her middle name, and her first name became Michaela. When she showed her mother the magazine picture, her mother smiled and said, "Home in America, you will dance."

Michaela started with ballet lessons once a week. Then, it became twice a week. Soon, Michaela was in the studio five times a week. Throughout her time in her local dance studio, students and parents questioned if she would ever succeed in ballet because of her "sport-like" figure, even though many of the White dancers had a similar body type to hers. On top of getting stares from her classmates just for being black, Michaela would get stares from other students concerning the patches on her skin. Despite the racism, discrimination, and challenges inherent in ballet, Michaela was still the same little girl who was so excited to see that ballerina on the magazine cover. This is what motivated her to keep going and to remain consistent.

With every step, arabesque, cabriole, and pirouette, Michaela put her all into her practice at the studio. Her consistency and diligence to continue dancing, overcome racial barriers, take on the literal pain of dance, and challenge orthodox standards of beauty and ballet allowed Michaela DePrince to eventually become a dancer with the Harlem Ballet. Later she even became a soloist at the Dutch National Ballet in the Netherlands.

EMBRACE THE UNCERTAINTY

As the saying goes, there are only two things that are certain in your life, and that is death and taxes. You're going to die. You might die today, tomorrow, or even in the next minute or so. Regardless of what country you live in, you're going to have to pay taxes. Besides those two things, everything else is going to be uncertain, and the best you can do is embrace the uncertainties that come your way.

So many people will share their successes on social media, but not everyone is going to talk about how they got to where they are today. It is rare that you will find people who are confident with the things that are uncertain. On social media, you follow people who create their own personal branding on things they're good at or to show off. It's so easy to compare yourself to "successful" people on Instagram. Don't be mistaken, though, because some people do have a genuine story, like Michaela DePrince, whose story I shared earlier in this chapter. You can't compare yourself to them. If anything, you can be inspired to motivate yourself to be consistent in your craft. But, what's important is that you stay true to your story and don't let the success of other people get in the way of your own.

YOU ARE EXACTLY WHERE YOU'RE SUPPOSED TO BE

When you look up at the sky on a warm spring day, watching birds soaring overhead is a beautiful sight. Although it may seem they know how to fly by pure instinct, birds must learn to fly like humans learn how to walk. As soon as a bird hatches from its egg, it's time for the bird to learn how to fly. The young bird will learn to fly by falling from the nest and making the long trip back. Altogether, this fledgling bird learning how to fly will eventually come to realize that if they fall from the nest, they'll be a lot more successful at flying. Once the bird realizes this, it'll spread its wings and begin flapping. After that, flapping eventually turns into flight. After a few weeks, the bird learns how to fly. The young bird is so proud of itself for all the work it put in and what it accomplished. Now imagine the mother bird goes up to the young bird and says, "Great job. But you were supposed to be able to learn how to fly the week before."

While you may recognize this as a pretty harsh reaction, this interaction is very similar to how we talk to ourselves in our own minds. This mother bird is the negative self-talk that we give ourselves when we don't complete our goals by our set deadlines. The worst part is that unless we actively decide to talk about what goes on inside our heads on a daily basis, then we can be completely mean to ourselves and the world may never know. This can even lead to a dangerous situation if we're not careful.

Rachel Hollis, author of *Girl, Wash Your Face,* said, "God has perfect timing." Regardless of your current age or what you believe in, know that whatever goals you strive for will happen when the time is right. With consistency and perseverance, you are more than capable of achieving your goals. If you've recently taken a break from your college classes, it is never too late to enroll again and finish that one class you have left to take. If you've just started your business, you can have zero clients for year one and then have one hundred thousand clients during year five. We live in a society that wants us to hit common milestones by a certain age, whether it's having kids by the age of thirty or moving out of your parents' home in your twenties. But even if none of the things I mentioned are things you want, well, that's cool too. What matters is that every time you want to achieve a new goal for your life, you stay consistent with your efforts over time. Regardless of whether it takes days, months, or years, it's going to be so rewarding to know you achieved your goal once it is all over. When you discover the power of patience, you can discover that you have the time for it.

YOU HAVE TIME FOR PATIENCE

While many people may know about American inventor Thomas Edison inventing the light bulb, not many know the number of attempts he needed to make just to get things right. Edison didn't work on perfecting the light bulb for only a few days. Thomas Edison attempted to perfect his invention many times. When he was asked about the process of inventing the light bulb during his seven hundredth time, he said, "I have not failed 700 times. I have not failed once. I have succeeded in proving that those 700 ways will not work. When I have eliminated the ways that will not work, I will find the way that will work." When he got the light bulb to his liking, it was during attempt number ten thousand.

From Thomas Edison, we can learn a lot about the power of patience. Although we may believe time is against us, it's time that is with us along our journeys. When you give yourself time to dedicate and master your craft, time enables you to unleash your talents and capabilities. As a result, you'll be able to make the world a better place with your talents. Psychologist, author, and speaker, Sherrie Campbell, said "Talent is long-earned patience. At the core of every true success is an awareness of the difficulties inherent in any achievement and the confidence that by persisting and being patient, something worthwhile will be realized." It's easy to want results quickly, but the results that come in the long-term are more meaningful.

To ensure you will earn the success you deserve, make sure you develop patience. One of the ways you can do this is through the "relaxation response" established by Herbert Benson in his book titled with the same name. The relaxation response is a response that can be used during physical and emotional stress as a result of impatience. The relaxation response occurs when you practice focused breathing for approximately twenty minutes each day. Twenty minutes may seem like a long time, but it's one of the best practices you can use when you combine it with the next method, which is to literally make yourself wait.

In a 2014 study conducted by the Association for Psychological Science, researchers discovered that when an individual waits for things, their happiness increases in the long run. Begin building your patience discipline by starting small. Ask yourself, do you really need your next package to arrive to your home in less than forty-eight hours? The next time you need to order something online, resist the urge to click on two-day shipping. Then, when your package does arrive, sit next to your package and practice the relaxation response for a minimum of twenty minutes. When the time is up, open your package. While this may seem silly, these small practices can prepare you to build your patience for larger-scale goals that require you to wait for results. Because once you're ready to take on your long-term goals, such as starting a business, for example, patience is going to help your state of mind when you don't see profits in the beginning of your journey. If you teach yourself the ability to be patient, you'll be able to believe in yourself and not give up on your dream just because of timing.

Lastly, once you get a grasp on developing patience, begin to develop gratitude. Each morning, when you wake up, become more observant. Be thankful you woke up. Throughout the day, observe all the good things that come your way, such as your bus coming on time, your friend telling you a funny joke, or you having a tasty lunch. When you acknowledge all of the amazing things that occur throughout the day, especially the people and environments that played a role in those things, you will experience a life that is more fulfilled. As a result, when you get more success to come your way, you'll appreciate it more because you are forcing your mind to focus on the positive more than the negative.

DON'T FORGET THE WHY

It may be difficult to practice patience at first, but it will become easier over time. The mind is trained to think of all new things as uncomfortable. When we do not get what we want right away, our minds freak out. But with your abilities, you're able to grow and develop to become patient while you're on your way to your success.

At this time, do not forget about the mission statement I mentioned in Chapter 10. Make sure you internalize your mission personal statement. Write it down in your notebook. Write it down on your Notes app on your phone. Make it your wallpaper with fancy font if you like because your mission statement should get you through all of your tough times in life.

When you don't see results right away, when you fail, and when you feel like the world is against you, look at your mission statement and remind yourself you are loved, you are strong, and you are brave. You matter and you are unique. That is a strength! Your experiences matter, and who you are is who you're meant to be, regardless of how long it takes you to do something. When you have your why at the forefront of your mind, there's no such thing as an impractical goal. That said, always be real with yourself. The most rewarding parts of your life result in consistency over time. Therefore, don't get all caught up on preset timelines because nothing happens overnight.

When things get tough, it's okay to be scared. It's okay not to know what to do. But don't get discouraged and give up just because there's a bump in the road. All of the amazing work you're doing right now is making a difference to someone, and you may not even realize it. Some people might be too shy to say it, but know that when you're patient, and you stay committed to your goals, people will pay attention and send good vibes your way. Be sure to follow through, stay patient, and know you have support.

TO-DO LIST
- Practice the relaxation response when your next package arrives at the door.
- Write a reflection on how the relaxation response worked for you.
- Practice gratitude by saying "I am thankful for..." the things that go on throughout your day.

FIND YOUR POWERS AND THEN POWER THE WORLD

———

"I believe there's a hero in all of us, that keeps us honest, gives us strength, makes us noble, and finally allows us to die with pride, even though sometimes we have to be steady, and give up the thing we want the most. Even our dreams."

—SPIDERMAN

Imagine you could be like Ish Verduzco, who found his dream job at just twenty-three years old.

In February 2018, that is exactly what happened when he began his role as a global events coordinator at LinkedIn. With a degree from the University of California, Merced, and coming from a Mexican-American household in Eastern Los Angeles, Ish knew he was living his ancestor's wildest dreams.

After finishing his orientation on the first day of his job, one of the first things that came to Ish's mind at the multibillion-dollar company was, "Holy shit. Am I the only one noticing that there are no people of color here?" Being one of the few people of color in his workplace, this was a real culture shock for Ish. As Ish is grabbing a snack from the office kitchen before heading back to work, someone taps him on his shoulder.

"Aye, what's up, *Compa*? You must be new to LinkedIn. Welcome! I'm Hector."

"Thank you. I'm Ish. Nice to meet you, Hector. You know where the other Latinos are at?"

"Well, there's not that many yet. But, don't worry. You and I are going to work on that."

The Spanglish made Ish feel at home, but after he went home that day, he wondered why things were the way they were. Working as one of the few people of color in a big tech company like LinkedIn was not easy for Ish. In a place where he was not represented, sometimes it felt like a lot of pressure. About two years later, he landed another role in the company as a global social media marketing lead. In his role, he was responsible for leading the social media for LinkedIn's largest customer-facing event, #TalentConnect, with headline speakers such as Gary Vee and Michelle Obama, being responsible for overseeing all of the social media accounts for the Talent Solutions team. And having to develop influencer marketing campaigns and working with marketers all over the world at LinkedIn, Ish knew his role would be challenging, but rewarding. On top of that, being one of the few people of color could have him in the spotlight and may determine what it will be like for others in his shoes who may come after him.

He would go to work each day, and soon, Ish was learning the ropes at the company, especially from Hector. Since Hector was senior in his career, whatever questions Ish had, Hector was more than happy to answer them. Being around ten years older than Ish and senior in his career at the company, Hector could connect Ish with extraordinary opportunities at LinkedIn. You would catch them heading from one big event to the next. After a while, Ish began to become recognizable by the company's leaders and other employees. Still, surely, Ish started to feel like he belonged at the prestigious tech company, even if he was one of the few.

But being one of the few, he eventually became his superpower.

As Ish continued to grow in his career at LinkedIn, he started going to more events during his spare time. During this entire time, it was important for Ish to remain true to himself and never forget about his community. In addition to Ish's role at LinkedIn, you would find Ish volunteering his time to speak to high school and college students from underrepresented communities. He also started hosting kids from East Oakland, where people of color don't have many opportunities. Because Ish was a younger employee at LinkedIn with a unique cultural background and coming from a place like

East LA resonated with the students Ish spoke to, his unique perspective allowed Ish to connect with different groups. This was when Ish realized that being one of the few became a superpower instead of it being odd. Internally at LinkedIn, not only was Ish being recognized for doing well in his role, but Ish was good at connecting and helping the community. Years later, those same kids who were eating and kicking it back with Ish for lunch would be seen at LinkedIn and similar companies, and Ish would be using his superpowers at Snap, Inc. writing his book, and eventually in his future entrepreneurial endeavors.

HOW DO I GET SUPERPOWERS?

In every superhero narrative, whether you are a Marvel fan, DC fan, or both, superheroes may have unique stories of how they specifically got their powers. Regardless of if they inherited their powers or had an encounter, superheroes have powers they choose to help power the world. Think about some of your favorite superheroes. Bruce Banner becomes the Hulk when he is exposed to gamma rays trying to save Rick Jones. Steve Rogers becomes Captain America after being infused with the super-soldier serum to help the United States win World War II. T'Challa gets his powers as the Black Panther with the heart-shaped herb from Wakanda. Wonder Woman gets her powers as a member of the Amazon. The list can go on and on. Regardless of how any superhero gets their powers, all superheroes use their superpowers to make the world a better place. Yet, while their powers tend to have some similarities, notice how each hero has unique traits and capabilities that make them individuals who stand out among the crowd.

As human beings living in the real world, we tend to stray away from acting as if we do not have "powers" because we don't want to associate ourselves with fantasy. Yet, we fail to understand that we are all superheroes. Our stories and experiences of how we find our true "superpowers" are going to be more mundane. It's not going to be as dramatic, and most of the time, it is not going to be life threatening (unless you're someone like Hal Elrod). What is true, though, is that all human beings have these incredible abilities to change the world. These abilities that people have spurred on the most influential accomplishments of humankind. These abilities allow us to solve the world's problems. Alex M. Wood from the University of Manchester completed a study on whether strengths lead to a better over-all quality of life for an individual. Based on the result of his study, people who utilized their strengths had greater levels of well-being in the long run. Those who participated in the study reported "greater self-esteem, vitality, and positive affect, and lower perceived stress." In other words, if you utilize the things you are good at, you're going to feel good about the life you live. And it only makes sense.

But remember when I said most of us don't know our super-powers? Why is that? Well, it is because our superpowers are not going to be easy to find. I said we either don't realize the powers we already have or have yet to discover our hidden superpowers. The first one is more knowing you like doing something or knowing you are good at something, but you probably don't think you can put this skill to use. The second one is more of you having to do more exploring to find things you like and are really good at. You have to figure out why you do not know your superpower, and the way you figure this out is by asking yourself the following:

WHAT IS SOMETHING I WANT TO LEARN?

Part of the journey to becoming your own superhero is gaining new skills along the way, and sometimes it's okay to take on a project to discover them. Think about things you would be interested in, whether it be how to code, how to invest, how to juggle, or even how to become a better dancer. Also, think about situations when you needed to respond to an interaction with someone. After reflecting on that experience, think about what better responses you can utilize in the future. There's no limit to how far you want to discover.

In Ish's journey at LinkedIn, there were many hard skills Ish utilized to be successful, such as marketing and social media. Those skills can be taught, and you can learn those skills through a course or online web browsing. In addition to listening to lectures, training, and attending workshops, you should practice as much as you can on your own time to eventually reach mastery. Ish, as a result of his upbringing as one of the few people of color at LinkedIn, has allowed him to find additional superpowers that eventually influence his other endeavors. When Ish begins to have lunches with younger kids from East Oakland, he learns that in addition to loving the job that requires him to become creative, he also likes to help the community.

From Ish's interest in helping his community, he learned a lot about communicating effectively to different audiences, which helped him connect with the kids who visited the office. Ish could unravel these skills because he was one of the few people at his company with his background, which led him to do things that utilized his background as a tool that not many employees at his job were doing. All these things that occurred in Ish's time at LinkedIn have allowed Ish to grow not just professionally but personally as well.

Superheroes combine their strengths to make the world a better place. Becoming your own superhero consists of learning your soft skills, hard skills, and reflecting on your experiences to unravel more superpowers. The difference between us real-life humans and the superheroes we see in movies and TV is that there's more opportunity to unravel more superpowers during the progression of our lives. The similarities are that becoming a superhero can come from bizarre circumstances. We must learn how to unravel these powers to make this world better than it was yesterday.

DISCOVER YOUR POWERS

Whether you have discovered your strengths are or not, know that everyone has strengths. People always have their moments when they are at their best. One of the ways this can be identified is with the Csikszentmihalyi's state of flow. As discussed earlier in Part 4, when you spend more time being focused on something compared to other activities, then it's a good sign that this activity is your strength. Stop what you're doing, and before you continue this chapter, create a long list of what you are good at. Based on those things you are good at, think of the soft skills that come out of those hard skills. If you are having trouble, phone a friend or family member and write down the things they tell you. Sometimes we can't also identify our own skills, but the people in our life can indicate the things we may not notice. Don't be afraid to utilize them!

Take time to explore these activities for your hard skills and develop on your skill set. However, what else is it that we can do to see where our strengths lie? The truth is, the journey to discovery will not just require self-reflection, but also the opinions of others. In order to discover your powers, sometimes we cannot see them with our own eyes. Rather, we need others to point them out.

One of the first things you need to do when trying to discover your strengths is that whatever you do not know, ask your close friends and family. They will be able to tell you a lot of things that can be an eye-opener. Compared to how you view yourself, people may point out some strengths that you may or may not have noticed. Gary Vaynerchuk, founder of Vayner Media, suggests that one of the ways you can see how others think of you is by mimicking how market research is collected. He says, "Take the five to ten people that know you the best. Split them into two categories: people you connect with on a deep level of love, and people who you are close with, but maybe you're a little different in lifestyle and personality. Then, ask one person from each category to honestly tell you what they think you're best at, and what they think you're worst at" When you do this, it is very similar to how market researchers develop a control group and an experimental group when conducting their projects. This allows you to get different perspectives on who you are and what capabilities people may recognize without having an overt amount of bias.

Secondly, just like superheroes, many of us can find our powers when we go out of our way to help people in our world. While most people will stay on the sidelines, superheroes take action by making situations better for themselves and others. To do this, find ways to help others through community service organizations. Community service not only allows you to build more hard skills in many different areas, but you will utilize your current skills, as well as soft skills within your disposal, to better your community. Western Connecticut State University recommends community service to everyone, especially young adults, because it encourages civic responsibility, strengthens your community, and develops overall esteem.

Being able to understand your powers enables you to do great things for yourself as well as the world. While we may not recognize our powers in the beginning, know it is okay to take time to discover them, especially if you need others to point you in the right direction. Because regardless of when you feel like you will be ready, it is time to let go of the fear of being ourselves and allow ourselves to let out our own expression of who we are.

TO DO LIST
- Identify your strengths.
- Ask your friends and loved ones what they believe your strengths are.
- Volunteer within your community.

CONCLUSION CHAPTER

———

Throughout my journey writing this book, I've had the opportunity to interview several entrepreneurs, educators, and professionals who have truly faced the odds of getting where they are today. Whether it was moving to the other side of the world, selling their car to save money for their next film production, or carving out space in the Broadway industry, they've all done what was necessary to get to where they wanted to be. Regardless of what their situation was, it was crucial they not only understood what their passion was but they also understood their value as a person.

They all accomplished great things because of this: They didn't ask for permission.

Many people require approval ratings from others to take next steps—and you can't blame them. Society was built on seeking approval ratings from others, from applying to colleges and jobs to posting on Instagram to get our likes and comments. Our minds are trained to get permission on almost everything. There may be people who recognize your talent and say things like, "You're really funny. You should be a comedian!" "You have a good idea. You should write a book!" Although comments such as these are nice to hear, they're just permission disguised as encouragement. Your mind can't tell the difference because of how accustomed you are to this permission-driven society.

When a problem occurs, it's in our DNA to look for a solution. But if a challenge comes up without a blueprint solution for you to use as a guide, give yourself the freedom to create your own solution. To make your solution, you can't ask for the permission of others. Whether you want to get your next degree, start a business, or write a book, you may want to ask for a person's advice on what you should do. Remember, although people can give good advice that can help you succeed, advice is only advice. And if you don't get the approval you want from others on your next project, start anyway, even if you don't initially have their support . People will not be genuinely willing to support you until they see the value of your work. You may want to ask for help or guidance right away, but people will be naturally more excited to help you once they see the value you bring to the table.

So how do you create value? You begin by creating your solution. If you are the first, it's okay to be afraid. But, do not be afraid to be the problem solver. If you're the first one to create a solution to a brand-new challenge, asking for permission will not get you far. Founders of successful companies don't ask for permission to start their business. I did not get permission to write this book from anyone. Instead, I just began researching and writing. Filmmakers start their next film by picking up their camera. Successful athletes start their journey by practicing the necessary skills. And for you, you begin your next solution by getting up and doing. When you utilize the capabilities of your mind, your skills, and your value, it's then you can take the world by storm. You don't need permission from the world on how you should live your life. To ensure you are getting the most out of your life, take risks, take care of yourself, and be able to commit to yourself. Do not be afraid to put yourself out in the world because the world is waiting for you to make your mark.

Do not wait until tomorrow, start today. You have what it takes to get your life where you want it to be. It requires risks and challenges, but in the end, it's gratifying. It starts with the uncomfortable. It starts by taking that first step and saying to yourself, "I can do this." When you wake up in the morning, count to five and get up. Do not snooze your alarm. Make a plan of what you need to do that day, and do not be afraid to try what is new just because you're a novice. It's essential that you remind yourself why you want to accomplish your goal and why you are the one responsible for bringing this to the universe. It's time to stop saying "one day." Instead, get into the habit of saying, "Day One."

ACKNOWLEDGMENTS

First and foremost, thank you. This book is nothing without readers. As there are so many things you can be doing with your time, I am thankful you had my book in your hand.

To all of those who have allowed me to share my story with you, I cannot thank you enough for lending an open ear. I would like to acknowledge my family, who have always reminded me to never give up.

To my friends who have pushed me to be my best self and believed in my vision, thank you.

A special shout-out to my best friends, Sydney Sullivan, Kennedy Jackson, Alana Hodges, and Tyler L. Thomas, for checking in on me during the late nights and early mornings.

Thank you to everyone at New Degree Press and Creator Institute for allowing me to have this opportunity. A special shout-out to my professor, Eric Koester; my DE, Stephanie Watson; my MRE, Bianca Myrtil; the head of NDP, Brian Bies;

and everyone else who has kept in constant communication with me to bring this book to life.

To all of those who I interviewed for this book, thank you for sharing your advice, your stories, your time, and your laughs with me. I have learned a lot from every single one of you:

Denise Soler Cox, Elizardi Castro, Ish Verduzco, Joe Michaels, Lawrence Drake II, PhD, Luis Salgado, Dr. Nido Qubein, Shonda Burrus, Son Han, Tiffany Haddish

Lastly, I'd like to acknowledge everyone who has preordered this book. Which, in turn, helped me cover the upfront costs of such a project:

Aleida Rojas, Amber Medero, Anam Munawar, Andrew J. Koehler, Andriw Read, Anna LoMonaco, Arnai Johnson, Audrey Avila, Austin Clark, Austin Perez Schoff, Belinda Pendergrass, Brittany DeJesus, Christian Talia, Christy Hribar, Corinna Fonseca, Crystallin Estrada, Cynthia Cruz, Dave Nelson, Debbie Gilner, Dennis Young, Dionne Herbert, Douglas Hall, Dr. Nido Qubein, Eduardo Valentin, Efrin Martinez, Elizabeth Veeser, Ena Pabon, Eric Koester, Erika Cabrera, Ernesto Arroyo, Evie Hernandez, Geneva Harrison, Gloria M. Estrada, Glory Nelson, Grace B Lesher, Harmony Leon, Ihsan Christie, Iris Nieves, Irisneri Alicea, Isabell Hernandez, Jamani A., Jayla Gulley, Jenny Trieu, Jessica Pomales, Josefina Gutierrez, Juan C. Estrada, Julissa Pabon, Julz Del Viscio, Kaelyn Thimons, Kamille Vargas, Karen Huezo, Kathy Mendoza, Katy Parisi, Kelly Thomas, Kennedy Jackson, Latasha Harrison, Lawrence Drake II, PhD, Leighla Henderson, Maizy Pareja, Manuel Figueroa, Maria (Zagry) Lopez, Marysol Ayala,

Matthew Steffens, Mayra Cruz, Michael Hernandez, Michael Morochnick, Miguel Hernandez, Mihaela Macioca, Miriam Lassalle Dodson, Nyla Hernandez, Omayra Pabon, Pablo Tejada, Rain Nelson, Raquel Gatling, Rashon Lance Jones, River Nelson, Robert Rainer MD, Rosita Vazquez, Salvatore Mangano, Sam Carr, Sam Shunney, Samantha Nieves, Sandra Hernandez, Sasha Miller, Savannah Hernandez, Sebastian Pabon, Shyquel Allison, Sky Nelson, Skye Dodson, Son Han, Sonaray Miller, Star Hernandez, Suleyma Torres, Taj Alston, Taylor Arthur, Terry Leon, Thanh-Thao (Sue) Do, TJ Foster, Tranaeé Jenkins, Tyler L. Thomas, Vizhnay, Will Coomer, Wynta Dodson

Because of all of you, I was able to make my dreams come true. I hope this book inspired you to rise up and go after your dreams, too.

Together We Rise,

Nia Rainer

APPENDIX

———

INTRODUCTION

Conklin, Justin. "New Year's Resolutions Are for Losers - Take These 4 Steps Instead." Forbes. Forbes Magazine, March 17, 2020. https://www.forbes.com/sites/justinconklin/2018/12/18/new-years-resolutions-are-for-loserstake-these-4-steps-instead/?sh=88da0e35e2cb.

CHAPTER 1

Ackerman, Courtney E. "What Is Gratitude and Why Is It So Important? [2019 Update]." PositivePsychology.com, February 5, 2021. https://positivepsychology.com/gratitude-appreciation/.

Brown, Robert J. *You Can't Go Wrong Doing Right: How a Child of Poverty Rose to the White House and Helped Change the World.* New York: Convergent, 2019.

OWN "Oprah on Taking Responsibility for Your Life | Oprah's Lifeclass | Oprah Winfrey Network." October 21, 2011. Video, 2:05. https://www.youtube.com/watch?v=Dp_cmLfJZ1w.

Tajfel, Henri, and John Turner. "Social Identity Theory." Social Identity Theory - Henri Tajfel and John Turner, 1979. http://www.age-of-the-sage.org/psychology/social/social_identity_theory.html

Thompson, Lisa. "#Thankful: Appreciate Your Struggles." *Self Love Beauty* (blog), November 25, 2015. https://selflovebeauty.wordpress.com/2015/11/25/thankful-appreciate-your-struggle./

Vandor, Peter, and Nikolaus Franke. "Why Are Immigrants More Entrepreneurial?" Harvard Business Review, September 21, 2017. https://hbr.org/2016/10/why-are-immigrants-more-entrepreneurial.

CHAPTER 2

Dweck, Carol. "The Power of Believing That You Can Improve." TED video, 10:11. https://www.ted.com/talks/carol_dweck_the_power_of_believing_that_you_can_improve.

Jim Harger. "James Baker III Recalls His White House Years after Serving Presidents Ford, Reagan and Bush." mlive, October 30, 2011. https://www.mlive.com/politics/2011/10/james_baker_iii_recalls_his_wh.html.

Mutel, Didier, and Isaac Newton. Philosophiae Naturalis Principia Mathematica. Paris: Atelier. Didier Mutel, 2011.

CHAPTER 3

Berg, Madeline. "America's Newest Beauty Billionaire Built an Empire Targeting Women's Eyebrows." Forbes, 2018. https://www.forbes.com/sites/maddieberg/2018/05/11/americas-newest-beauty-billionaire-built-an-empire-targeting-womens-eyebrows/?sh=515bbf5e60d9.

Bias, Lauren Maillian. The Path Redefined: Getting to the Top on Your Own Terms. Benbella Books, 2015.

Dictionary.com. s.v "Versatility (n.)." Accessed June 1, 2021. https://www.dictionary.com/browse/versatility.

"Market Positioning - Creating an Effective Positioning Strategy." Corporate Finance Institute, July 16, 2020. https://corporatefinanceinstitute.com/resources/knowledge/strategy/market-positioning/.

CHAPTER 4

Hammen, Constance, and Shannon Daley. "Poor Interpersonal Problem Solving as a Mechanism of Stress Generation in Depression among Adolescent Women." Journal of Abnormal Psychology. U.S. National Library of Medicine. https://pubmed.ncbi.nlm.nih.gov/8530761/.

Kevin Durant, "A Quote by Kevin Durant," Goodreads (Goodreads). https://www.goodreads.com/quotes/699064-hard-work-beats-talent-when-talent-fails-to-work-hard.

Manson, Mark. The Subtle Art of Not Giving a F*CK A Counterintuitive Approach to Living a Good Life. HarperLuxe, 2019.

CHAPTER 5

Bravata, Dena, Divya Madhusudhan, Michael Boroff, and Kevin Cokley. "Commentary: Prevalence, Predictors, and Treatment of Imposter Syndrome: A Systematic Review." Journal of Mental Health & Clinical Psychology 4, no. 3 (2020): 12–16. https://doi.org/10.29245/2578-2959/2020/3.1207.

Clance, Pauline Rose, and Suzanne Ament Imes. "The Imposter Phenomenon in High Achieving Women: Dynamics and Therapeutic Intervention." *Psychotherapy: Theory, Research & Practice* 15, no. 3 (1978): 241–247. https://doi.org/10.1037/h0086006.

Sakulku, Jaruwan. "The Impostor Phenomenon." *The Journal of Behavioral Science* 6, no. 1 (2011): 75–97. https://doi.org/10.14456/ijbs.2011.6.

CHAPTER 6

Emmons, Robert. "Why Gratitude Is Good." *Greater Good Magazine*, 2010. https://greatergood.berkeley.edu/article/item/why_gratitude_is_good#:~:text=%20What%20good%20is%20gratitude%3F%20%201%20Gratitude,showing%20that%20in%20the%20face%20of...%20More%20.

Reffkin, Robert. *No One Succeeds Alone: Learn Everything You Can from Everyone You Can.* Boston: Houghton Mifflin Harcourt, 2021.

TEDx Talks. "Ask and You Will Achieve | Denise Fay | TEDxDrogheda." October 27, 2016. 7:45 https://www.youtube.com/watch?v=J93IPj_2ke4.

Zetlin, Minda. "Five Reasons You Must Learn to Ask for Help." *Inc.* https://www.inc.com/minda-zetlin/5-reasons-you-must-learn-to-ask-for-help.html.

CHAPTER 7

"Depression: What Is Burnout?" InformedHealth.org [Internet]. U.S. National Library of Medicine, June 18, 2020. https://www.ncbi.nlm.nih.gov/books/NBK279286/.

Fraga, Juli. "How to Identify and Prevent Burnout." Healthline. Healthline Media, May 18, 2019. https://www.healthline.com/health/tips-for-identifying-and-preventing-burnout.

Huffington, Arianna Stassinopoulos. *The Sleep Revolution: Transforming Your Life, One Night at a Time.* New York: Harmony Books, 2017.

Levy, Marc. *If Only It Were True.* New York: Pocket Books, 2000.

Pencavel, John. "The Productivity of Working Hours." *IZA*, April 2014. http://ftp.iza.org/dp8129.pdf.

"Stress Relief: When and How to Say No." *Mayo Clinic Health* (blog), March 28, 2019. https://www.mayoclinic.org/healthy-lifestyle/stress-management/in-depth/stress-relief/art-20044494#:~:text=%20Here%20are%20some%20things%20to%20keep%20in,out%20of%20an%20obligation.%20The%20truth...%20More%20.

Stuckey, Heather L., and Jeremy Nobel. "The Connection Between Art, Healing, and Public Health: A Review of Current Literature." *American Journal of Public*

Health 100, no. 2 (2010): 254–63.
https://doi.org/10.2105/ajph.2008.156497.

Sussex Publishers, LLC. "Burnout." n.d. 2021.
https://www.psychologytoday.com/us/basics/burnout.

Vaynerchuk, Gary. *#AskGaryVee: One Entrepreneur's Take on Leadership, Social Media, and Self-Awareness.* HarperCollins, n.d.

Wigert, Ben, and Sangeeta Agrawal. "Employee Burnout, Part 1: The 5 Main Causes." Gallup.com. Gallup, June 14, 2021.
https://www.gallup.com/workplace/237059/employee-burnout-part-main-causes.aspx.

CHAPTER 8

Butler, Lisa D. "Self-Care Starter Kit[SM]." Self-Care Starter Kit[SM] - University at Buffalo School of Social Work - University at Buffalo. University of Buffalo, February 8, 2021.
http://socialwork.buffalo.edu/resources/self-care-starter-kit.html.

Davis, Tchiki. "Self-Care: 12 Ways to Take Better Care of Yourself." *Psychology Today.* Sussex Publishers, December 2018.
https://www.psychologytoday.com/us/blog/click-here-happiness/201812/self-care-12-ways-take-better-care-yourself.

Glowiak, Matthew. "What Is Self-Care and Why Is It Important for You?" *Southern New Hampshire University*, 2020.
https://www.snhu.edu/about-us/newsroom/2019/04/what-is-self-care.

Hodges, Lauren. "How to Start Therapy." NPR. NPR, January 23, 2020.
https://www.npr.org/2019/12/11/787058888/how-to-start-therapy.

Johnson, Joseph. "Daily Number of e-Mails Worldwide 2025." Statista. April 7, 2021.
https://www.statista.com/statistics/456500/daily-number-of-e-mails-worldwide/.

Koetsier, John. "Covid Boosted Retail Subscriptions up to 145%: The New Retail Therapy?" *Forbes.* Forbes Magazine, July 20, 2020.
https://www.forbes.com/sites/johnkoetsier/2020/07/19/covid-boosted-retail-subscriptions-up-to-145-the-new-retail-therapy/?sh=3c04879e15d1.

McMains, S., and S. Kastner. "Interactions of Top-down and Bottom-up Mechanisms in Human Visual Cortex." *Journal of Neuroscience* 31, no. 2 (2011): 587–597.
https://doi.org/10.1523/jneurosci.3766-10.2011.

Weaver, Elizabeth A., and Hilary H. Doyle. "How Does Exercise Affect the Brain?" Dana Foundation. Dana Foundation, March 24, 2020.
https://www.dana.org/article/how-does-exercise-affect-the-brain/.

"Your Personal Appearance and How It Affects Your Self-Esteem." *Get Hair* (blog), May 15, 2020.
https://gethair.co.uk/blog/hairloss-self-esteem/.

CHAPTER 9

"About Tesla." Tesla, n.d. https://www.tesla.com/about.

Andrews, Andy. "7 Proven Keys to Success (and How to Use Them in Your Life)." *Https://Www.andyandrews.com/*(blog), June 1, 2017. https://www.andyandrews.com/keys-to-success/.

Canfield, Jack, Mark Victor Hansen, and Amy Newmark. *Chicken Soup for the Soul: Reader's Choice 20th Anniversary Edition: The Chicken Soup for the Soul Stories That Changed Your Lives.* Cos Cob, CT: Chicken Soup for the Soul Publishing, 2013.

Dictionary.com. s.v. "Purpose (n.)." Accessed June 1, 2021. https://www.dictionary.com/browse/purpose.

"GET HELP." What Is Nike's Mission? | Nike Help, n.d. https://www.nike.com/help/a/nikeinc-mission.

Habersberger, Keith, Ned Fulmer, Eugene Lee Yang, and Zach Kornfeld. *The Hidden Power of F*Cking Up.* New York, NY: Dey Street Books, 2019.

"Starbucks Mission Statement 2021: Starbucks Mission & Vision Analysis." Starbucks Mission Statement 2021 | Starbucks Mission & Vision Analysis, January 27, 2021. https://mission-statement.com/starbucks/.

Verduzco, Ish. *How Successful People Get Ish Done - A 7 Step Framework to Achieve Your Goals.* Amazon Publishing, 2020.

Zimmerman, Alan R. *The Payoff Principle: Discover the 3 Secrets for Getting What You Want out of Life and Work.* Austin, TX: Greenleaf Book Group Press, 2015.

CHAPTER 10

Barua, Nikki, and Monica Marquez. "Episode 148: Never Stop Learning." April, 2021. In *Beyond Barriers.* Produced by Gillian Donovan. Podcast, MP3 audio, 11:24. https://open.spotify.com/episode/47wTOimQgv6pALqwIcg24d?si=kZqQH1bJTL qcx-nAggJ5-Q

Csikszentmihalyi, Mihaly. *Flow: The Psychology of Optimal Experience.* New York: Harper and Row, 2009.

Hanselman, Yeager D. "A National Experiment Reveals Where a Growth Mindset Improves Achievement." *Nature,* no. 579 (2019): 368–370. https://pubmed.ncbi.nlm.nih.gov/31391586/.

Tseng, Julie, and Jordan Poppenk. "Brain Meta-State Transitions Demarcate Thoughts across Task Contexts Exposing the Mental Noise of Trait Neuroticism." *Nature Communications,* July 13, 2020. https://www.nature.com/articles/s41467-020-17255-9.

CHAPTER 11

Bailenson, Jeremy, and Laura L. Carstensen. "Connecting to the Future Self: Using Web-Based Virtual Reality to Increase Retirement Saving." Stanford Health Policy, Stanford University, Stanford, CA, 2011. https://healthpolicy.fsi.stanford.edu/research/connecting_to_the_future_self_using_webbased_virtual_reality_to_increase_retirement_saving.

Darmawangsa, Jade. (video) June 3, 2021 https://www.tiktok.com/@jadedarmawangsa/video/6969715309062245638?lang=en&is_copy_url=0&is_from_webapp=v1&sender_device=pc&sender_web_id=6905068656931063302.

Edelson, Paula. *A To Z of American Women in Sports.* New York: Facts on File, 2002.

Robbins, Mel. *The 5 Second Rule: Transform Your Life, Work, and Confidence with Everyday Courage.* Post Hill Press, 2017.

Sivers, Derek. "Keep Your Goals to Yourself." Filmed July 2010 in Oxford, United Kingdom TED video, 2:59. https://www.ted.com/talks/derek_sivers_keep_your_goals_to_yourself.

CHAPTER 12

Benson, Herbert. *The Relaxation Response.* New York: William Morrow, 1976.

Campbell, Sherrie. "8 Ways Practicing Patience Radically Increases Your Capacity for Success." Entrepreneur. September 3, 2015. https://www.entrepreneur.com/article/250211.

Edison, Thomas A. "Thomas A. Edison Quote: 'I Have Not Failed 700 Times...'," 2021. https://quotefancy.com/quote/916544/Thomas-A-Edison-I-have-not-failed-700-times-I-have-not-failed-once-I-have-succeeded-in.

Hollis, Rachel. *Girl, Wash Your Face: Stop Believing the Lies about Who You Are so You Can Become Who You Were Meant to Be.* Nashville, TN: Nelson Books, an imprint of Thomas Nelson, 2020.

Kumar, Amit, Matthew A. Killingsworth, and Thomas Gilovich. "Waiting for Merlot: Anticipatory Consumption of Experiential and Material Purchases." *Psychological Science* 25, no. 10 (October 2014): 1924–1931. https://doi.org/10.1177/0956797614546556.

Myers, Carrie. *Michaela DePrince: From War-Torn Childhood to Ballet Fame.* North Mankato, MN: Capstone Press, 2021.

CHAPTER 13

Vaynerchuk, Gary. "4 Ways to Find Out What Your Strengths Are." *Garyvaynerchuk.com* (blog), December 5, 2015. https://www.garyvaynerchuk.com/4-ways-to-find-out-what-your-strengths-are/.

Western Connecticut State University. "Community Service: Top 10 Reasons to Volunteer." Community Engagement, 2020. https://www.wcsu.edu/community-engagement/tips-for-volunteer/#:~:text=1%20 You%20make%20a%20difference.%202%20Volunteering%20encourages,It%20 brings%20people%20together.%20...%20More%20items...%20.

Wood, Alex M., P. Alex Linley, John Maltby, Todd B. Kashdan, and Robert Hurling. "Using Personal and Psychological Strengths Leads to Increases in Well-Being over Time: A Longitudinal Study and the Development of the Strengths Use Questionnaire." *Personality and Individual Differences* 50, no. 1 (2011): 15–19. https://doi.org/10.1016/j.paid.2010.08.004.